BLENDED

VOCABULARY for K–12 Classrooms

Harnessing the Power of Digital Tools and Direct Instruction

Kimberly A. Tyson   Angela B. Peery

Solution Tree | Press

a division of
Solution Tree

555 North Morton Street
Bloomington, IN 47404
800.733.6786 (toll free) / 812.336.7700
FAX: 812.336.7790

email: info@SolutionTree.com
SolutionTree.com

Visit **go.SolutionTree.com/literacy** to download the free reproducibles in this book.

Printed in the United States of America

21 20 19 18 17   2 3 4 5

Library of Congress Control Number: 2016955562

ISBN: 978-0-9913748-3-0 (paperback)

Solution Tree

Jeffrey C. Jones, CEO
Edmund M. Ackerman, President

Solution Tree Press

President and Publisher: Douglas M. Rife
Editorial Director: Tonya Maddox Cupp
Managing Production Editor: Caroline Weiss
Senior Production Editor: Tara Perkins
Senior Editor: Amy Rubenstein
Copy Chief: Sarah Payne-Mills
Copy Editor: Miranda Addonizio
Proofreader: Jessi Finn
Text and Cover Designer: Laura Cox
Editorial Assistants: Jessi Finn and Kendra Slayton

This book is dedicated to my two children, Taylor-Ruth and Corbin. You have taught me more about the meaning of life and love than you will ever know. To my wonderful parents, Willard and Ruth Tyson, who have always believed in me. Your unwavering love, support, and encouragement continue to shape who I am. And, to my best friends and sisters, Charleen and Heather.

—Kimberly

As we were finishing this book, one of our greatest American authors passed away. Pat Conroy was a master of words—and he was a friend. Every time I spoke with Pat, he wanted to know more about my job and about all the teachers with whom I was working. He revered teachers and paid homage to them in every book he wrote. So I dedicate this book to the memory of Pat Conroy, and I hope I'm doing his memory some small justice by supporting teachers with the ideas within.

—Angela

Acknowledgments

This book might not have been written had Claudia Wheatley, an educator and professional matchmaker of sorts, not introduced Kimberly and Angela. From there, the book that Kimberly envisioned took shape alongside Angela's expertise, knowledge, and experience. Claudia knows a good match when she sees one, and Kimberly and Angela both thank her.

Kimberly would like to thank two specific groups of dedicated teachers and instructional coaches: first, the teachers at Garden City Elementary School (Indianapolis, Indiana), who continue to work diligently to improve vocabulary instruction, particularly to meet the needs of English learners; and second, the K–12 Literacy Leadership Team at Zionsville Community Schools (Zionsville, Indiana), who not only dug deep to understand and implement the tiered vocabulary framework but also helped lead schoolwide implementation efforts. In addition, Kimberly thanks the many teachers, instructional coaches, principals, and administrators she has been privileged to work with and support to help refine effective vocabulary instruction. Their diligent instruction and feedback have helped shape her thinking and have made this resource more useful for others.

Angela would like to thank teachers Casey Rice and Ann Twigg for sharing examples of word walls and other vocabulary displays. Angela is also indebted to the teachers at Zwolle Elementary School (Zwolle, Louisiana) and McGuire College (Shepparton, Australia) for helping her explore effective vocabulary instruction in the context of their classrooms and their students. Lastly, Angela thanks Ginger Williams Garner for her unwavering support and for access to her students at Robert Smalls International Academy (Beaufort, South Carolina).

Solution Tree Press would like to thank the following reviewers:

Tracy S. Bailey
Chief Executive Officer
Freedom Readers™
    After School Literacy Program
Myrtle Beach, South Carolina

Melissa Biggerstaff
Associate Executive Director
Green River Regional
    Educational Cooperative
Bowling Green, Kentucky

Tonia Carriger
Program Coordinator
School on Wheels
Indianapolis, Indiana

Laura Frost
English Teacher
Nevada Virtual Academy
Las Vegas, Nevada

Chris Grissom
Associate Professor,
    Exceptional Needs Education
Marian University
Indianapolis, Indiana

Dana Johansen
Fifth-Grade Teacher
Greenwich Academy
Greenwich, Connecticut

Sarah Ledon
High School Instructional Coach
Nevada Virtual Academy
Las Vegas, Nevada

Maryellen Leelman
Speech/Language Pathologist
Lexington Public Schools
Lexington, Massachusetts

Carol Lutz
Consultant
Kokomo, Indiana

Ann Sweeney
Former Sixth-Grade Teacher
Greensburg, Indiana

Visit **go.SolutionTree.com/literacy** to
download the free reproducibles in this book.

Table of Contents

Reproducibles are in italics.

About the Authors

 **Kimberly A. Tyson, PhD,** "Dr. Kimberly," as she is known by many, has served as a classroom teacher, college administrator and instructor, and literacy consultant across the United States in classrooms ranging from preschool to twelfth grade. Kimberly contributes literacy insights regularly at *Dr. Kimberly's Literacy Blog* (www.kimberlytyson.com). She has written classroom curriculum and language arts sections of standardized assessments, and recently chaired the Elementary Reading National Evaluation Preparation Committee for Pearson Education. Kimberly is past president of several professional organizations and actively participates in contributing to the profession.

Over the years, Kimberly has joined with teachers, principals, and administrators to improve literacy in readers of all ages. Through The Literacy Lens Audit®, a research-based literacy audit she developed, Kimberly guided literacy leaders in assessing and improving curriculum, instruction, environment, and student achievement across schools and districts. In addition, Kimberly has worked with educational organizations, such as the I-READ Department of Education literacy improvement program, and educational service centers. She has also supported statewide initiatives.

Kimberly earned her doctorate from the University of Missouri–Kansas City. She discovered her love of word learning and vocabulary when working with middle and high school students in several initiatives within Kansas City Public Schools. Since then, vocabulary improvement has been the focus of much of her work alongside educators in schools and districts across the United States.

Kimberly's family includes two children, Taylor-Ruth and Corbin, and one rescue dog, Sally Girl. In her free time, she enjoys gardening, bicycling, knitting, and reading. To learn more about Kimberly's work, visit www.kimberlytyson.com or follow @tysonkimberly on Twitter.

 **Angela B. Peery, EdD,** is a consultant and author with three decades of experience as an educator. Since 2004, she has made more than one thousand presentations and has authored or co-authored eleven books. Angela has consulted with educators to improve teacher collaboration, formative assessment, effective instruction, and literacy across the curriculum. In addition to her consulting work, she is a former instructional coach, high school administrator, graduate-level education professor, and English teacher at the middle school, high school, and college levels. Her wide range of experiences allows her to work shoulder to shoulder with colleagues in any setting to improve educational outcomes.

Angela has been a Courage to Teach fellow and an instructor for the National Writing Project. She maintains memberships in several national and international education organizations and is a frequent presenter at their conferences. Her book *The Data Teams Experience: A Guide for Effective Meetings* (2011) supports the work of professional learning communities, and her most recent publications and consulting work highlight the importance of teaching academic vocabulary.

A Virginia native, Angela earned her bachelor's degree in English at Randolph-Macon Woman's College, her master's degree in liberal arts at Hollins College, and her doctorate at the University of South Carolina. Her professional licensures include secondary English, secondary administration, and gifted and talented education. She has also studied presentation design and delivery with expert Rick Altman. In 2015, she engaged in graduate study in brain-based learning.

To learn more about Angela's work, visit www.drangelapeery.com or follow @drangelapeery on Twitter.

To book Kimberly A. Tyson or Angela B. Peery for professional development, contact pd@SolutionTree.com.

Introduction

Today's world seems to move at the speed of light, and schools are no exception. The academic expectations for students zoom higher, high-stakes and low-stakes testing consume precious instructional hours, and teachers are increasingly conflicted about exactly what to teach and how best to do so. Educational policies will continue to shift and change the K–12 landscape; however, the importance of vocabulary will remain constant. Vocabulary and word knowledge are essential, serving as the basic building blocks of language and impacting fluency, comprehension, and achievement.

Vocabulary and Achievement in School and Beyond

First, to be clear, let's begin with a working definition of vocabulary. *Vocabulary*, in its simplest form, refers to the words we use to communicate effectively when we listen, speak, read, and write. Going a layer deeper, vocabulary is often divided into two broad categories that are useful for discussing words and word usage: receptive and expressive vocabulary. *Receptive vocabulary* refers to those words we understand when we listen and read, and *expressive vocabulary* refers to the words we use when speaking and writing. One's receptive vocabulary is much broader than one's expressive vocabulary. For example, a two-year-old child understands when his parent tells him that it's time to go outside to play, and since it's cold he'll need to bundle up in a coat, mittens, and a scarf. More than likely, the toddler will run to the closet and pull out his coat, mittens, and scarf even though he may not be able to verbalize this himself. Similarly, students understand many more specific words that you use within classroom discussions than they use when speaking and writing. Our overarching goal in vocabulary instruction is to help you move words in students' receptive banks to their expressive banks through direct instruction, indirect instruction, and the use of digital tools and games to review and practice with words. It's only through accurate use of new words that students add them to their personal lexicons.

A robust vocabulary helps students achieve success. Students must encounter new words in order to build their vocabulary and their knowledge of various concepts. Conceptual understanding, along with both general and specific word knowledge, impacts learning at every level. In addition, when older students know the meaning of specific words and are able to put related words together during a unit of study, they can connect to new content more readily and remember more (Marzano & Simms, 2013). Conversely, students who are deficient in vocabulary face numerous obstacles. Their reading range is limited, their writing lacks specificity and voice, and their spoken language lacks range of word choice and may give others a negative or inaccurate first impression.

It is not only for the purpose of individual growth and achievement that we teachers need to address vocabulary learning more directly than we have in the past. Many educators are familiar with the various research studies that correlate low literacy with poverty, unemployment, and incarceration (Baer, Kutner, Sabatini, & White, 2009; Hart & Risley, 2003). While we certainly want each student we teach to reach his or her full potential, there is also a large-scale, societal benefit when students increase their literacy. Literate adults are more likely to be employed, so they contribute to the economy through expenditures and taxes. They are also more likely to be well educated, and this bodes well for their families, as well-educated parents provide social and material advantages to their children. During the Great Recession in the United States, those with higher levels of education fared best—an outcome tied to literacy success (Rampell, 2013). Well-honed literacy skills provide a cushion against many types of hardship in a person's life. Effective vocabulary instruction is an integral piece of the puzzle that can help the young people we see every day in our classrooms become literate for life.

Vocabulary and Reading Comprehension

Vocabulary and its interconnected relationship with comprehension has been the focus of a great deal of research—both quantitative and qualitative—over many years. Decades of research reveal that vocabulary knowledge strongly correlates to reading comprehension. Landmark studies such as Frederick B. Davis's (1944, 1968) factor analysis and reanalysis by others (Spearritt, 1972; Thurstone, 1946) reveal that adults who have greater word knowledge and score high on vocabulary tests also score high on tests of reading comprehension. In other words, even though reading comprehension is a complex process, word knowledge plays the most important role.

Vocabulary and word knowledge also play an important role in comprehension for students. It is so critical to comprehension that the National Reading Panel (2000) includes vocabulary as one of the five essential components—or building blocks—of reading. Vocabulary and comprehension are so commingled that the National Reading Panel (2000) reports that separating them "is difficult, if not impossible" (p. 239).

Early vocabulary development is critical, and research shows that a lack of word knowledge has lingering effects. For example, kindergarten students' word knowledge predicts reading comprehension in second grade (Catts, Fey, Zhang, & Tomblin, 1999; Roth, Speece, & Cooper, 2002). Similarly, other researchers (Wagner, Muse, & Tannenbaum, 2007) find the same predictive ability persists from kindergarten to fourth grade. Perhaps even more surprisingly, Anne Cunningham and Keith Stanovich (1997) find that first-grade students' vocabulary knowledge predicts their reading comprehension level even later, in the eleventh grade.

Not only is vocabulary knowledge important for comprehension, it also relates to one's skills in writing. A student who reads frequently and possesses a large and varied vocabulary has many more words to choose from when writing. Although research on the connections between vocabulary and writing is sparse, one study shows that students who receive instruction in word consciousness use a greater number of rare words in their writing after instruction than before (Scott, Jamieson-Noel, & Asselin, 2003). The number of words a student knows greatly influences his or her verbal output, which is one of the first things other people, including teachers, notice. If you and your colleagues have discussed voice and word choice in writing with students, you likely know from experience that the best papers are the ones in which students use the most precise and specific words. These data all illustrate that students who enter school with deficient vocabulary knowledge seem to remain deficient.

Vocabulary Gaps and Literacy

Betty Hart and Todd R. Risley (2003), in their study of the vocabulary growth of three-year-old children from low-income families compared with toddlers from middle-class and professional families, find a stark and persistent difference in vocabulary knowledge and word acquisition between these groups. Hart and Risley (1995) estimate that students from professional families have been exposed to thirty million more words by age three than their low-income counterparts.

Some may wonder how such a large gap exists. In varied home settings, children's language experience differs both in quality and number of words heard. For example, professional parents more routinely engage with their children, using a variety of more sophisticated words and a broader array of words than working-class and low-income parents (Hart & Risley, 1995). Hart and Risley (1995) note that children of professional families enter school with a vocabulary of about 1,100 words, whereas children of working-class families enter knowing about 700 words, and children of welfare families have only amassed about 500 words upon entering school. Simply put, young children's language and social interactions closely mirror those of their parents. Putting it another way, "to grow up as the child of well-educated parents in an affluent American home is to hit the verbal lottery" (Pondiscio, 2014).

Unfortunately, the vocabulary gap in preschool-age children often starts them off in a game of catch up and keep up that compounds as they learn to read and later when they encounter increasingly difficult academic content. A large oral vocabulary helps students as they begin learning to read. Students with larger vocabularies tend to become better readers, enjoy reading more, and read independently with more frequency than students with smaller vocabularies, who struggle as readers and dislike reading (Stahl, 1999). Whether you teach upper elementary, middle, or high school, we suspect you know far too well the moans and groans of some of your students when independent reading time rolls around or textbook reading is required. Struggling readers actively seek to decrease their time and engagement with all sorts of text, trapping themselves in a world of simplistic vocabulary, limited content knowledge, and a distaste for reading for pleasure or information.

In addition, those students with broad vocabularies read more independently, which, in turn, exposes them further to words and additional vocabulary growth (Stanovich, 1986). Frequently referred to as the *Matthew effect* (Figurelli, 2015), reading volume makes a difference not only in terms of acquiring reading skills but also in deepening and broadening an individual's word knowledge (Fielding, Wilson, & Anderson, 1986; Nagy, Herman, & Anderson, 1985). And, of critical importance to learning, one's vocabulary knowledge directly relates to reading comprehension. To sum it up, the "rich get richer" (Stanovich, 1986, p. 380).

We know vocabulary and word knowledge gaps widen as students mature through the grades. Research supports the urgency we should feel to positively influence our students' understanding of a broad range of words. Given the importance of vocabulary, one would reason that schools would emphasize a comprehensive approach to vocabulary development—one that would shore up deficits and build students' word knowledge. Yet, historically, schools have not done so (Blachowicz, Fisher, Ogle, & Watts-Taffe, 2006). For as much as we know about the positive effects of equipping students with a wide vocabulary, well-meaning teachers typically provide little more than a cursory nod to word meanings and often simply mention synonyms when defining a word or refer students to the dictionary (Scott et al., 2003). Both of these methods are insufficient to build the vocabulary students need to become capable readers.

Therefore, we are proposing a blended vocabulary model that consists of several components: modeling, explicit instruction, and orchestration of incidental learning opportunities. Use of online tools and digital applications runs throughout all components. This model honors other models of vocabulary instruction, is grounded in research, and utilizes modern technologies.

About This Book

In spite of decades of research on vocabulary and word learning, many of the practical aspects of that research have failed to trickle down to classroom instructional practice. As we've noted, persistent gaps in students' vocabulary knowledge affect their comprehension and therefore their overall academic achievement. We have seen the ways academic achievement, or lack thereof, further affects students' futures beyond the classroom. It's imperative that we address these gaps and deliver direct instruction to all students to expand their vocabulary acquisition and ensure their learning and future success. We seek to address these gaps within these pages. Our goal in writing this book is straightforward. Within this professional resource, we seek to provide K–12 educators with a research-based, practical guide to more clearly understand vocabulary learning and its important implications for classroom instruction.

Word learning occurs through many varied avenues—reading, discussion, listening, environmental print, games, and direct instruction, to name just a few. Today, technology offers new avenues for practice, review, and word learning, and the Common Core State Standards (CCSS) for English language arts advocate using digital technology to support domain-specific literacy in secondary classrooms (National Governors Association Center for Best Practices [NGA] & Council of Chief State School Officers [CCSSO], 2010). This book seeks to inform and expand educator understanding around a blended learning framework that harnesses the power of digital tools to reinforce and expand effective, practical word learning in the classroom. We share instructional strategies for word learning for students of all ages and varying abilities. Integrating digital technology into instruction can help bridge the gap between students' out-of-school and in-school practices (Alvermann, 2008; Hinchman, Alvermann, Boyd, Brozo, & Vacca, 2003/2004). Note that not every strategy we share will be conducive to digital tool use, nor should it be. Curriculum standards, along with your instructional decisions, come first in the planning cycle. You can then select technology and digital tools to support specific standards and instructional goals. In other words, it's not about the technology but rather the teaching and learning that occur both inside and outside the classroom. We offer this simple yet meaningful model to help you better equip students for greater command over the power of words.

Intended Audience

When we write and create resources, we think about those who will likely read the book or blog post or use the resources. While our primary audience is teachers and literacy leaders, other individuals may also benefit from the information about vocabulary learning within this book. Though these roles vary in respect to implementing standards and vocabulary, each is nonetheless important. Our overarching goal is to provide educators with greater understanding specific to selecting, teaching, and assessing vocabulary that will give them the knowledge they need to implement a school- or districtwide comprehensive vocabulary model. To do so requires involvement from all these individuals.

- **Teachers:** Those who directly teach students in K–12 classrooms will benefit from the straightforward definitions and practical examples; instructional implications; instructional strategies for elementary, secondary, and special populations; and resources found within this book and online. We've observed that teachers often have a difficult time integrating digital tools to support literacy instruction. However, as responsible teachers, we must prepare students to become literate in using digital technology to support their independent learning and ultimate success in higher education and the workplace. Throughout this book, we provide guidance for you on using digital tools for instruction as well as for professional development and collaboration.
- **Literacy leadership teams and collaborative teams:** This book supports in-depth study and conversation about best vocabulary practices. We've included next steps at the close of every chapter that you can use to support a book study and to help implement research-based, instructional practices. We'd be thrilled

to join you in a Twitter chat or other online forum should you choose to have an online book study.

- **Principals and district leaders:** This resource provides the nuts and bolts for you as building and district leaders to select, teach, and assess vocabulary across classrooms. Specific to your role, we also address how to build and sustain a culture of word learning, which we have found critical for sustainable implementation and success.
- **Instructional coaches:** This book is designed to support your efforts as the individual who trains and supports teachers. You can easily divide this resource into manageable chunks of content suitable for staff meetings, professional learning days, or meetings with grade-level teams or professional learning communities. Additionally, many of the blog posts we refer to throughout the book can serve as online resources providing additional examples, images, and resources.

What You Can Expect From This Book

Vocabulary plays an undeniable role in the reading success of students. The NGA and the CCSSO's Common Core State Standards, along with many state and provincial standards, emphasize the role of vocabulary and word learning. Students who continually build a broad, enriched vocabulary become abler learners and achieve at higher levels than those who don't. As educators who support teachers, we firmly believe that learning more about effective vocabulary instruction and refining current practices deserve our attention. The chapters that follow provide information and strategies for implementing effective school- or districtwide vocabulary instruction.

In chapter 1, we begin by discussing the importance of establishing a culture of word learning and providing guidance for literacy leadership teams to begin this work in their schools and districts. Chapter 2 details our proposed blended vocabulary model for conducting intentional vocabulary instruction, outlining other valuable instructional models we have drawn from. We provide background information about tiered vocabulary words and suggestions for ways you can approach the task of choosing the vocabulary words teachers will teach in their classrooms in chapter 3. Chapter 4 then explains effective instructional and assessment methods to teach and evaluate students' vocabulary knowledge. Chapters 5 and 6 provide several specific strategies you may employ in elementary and secondary classrooms, respectively, to intentionally teach vocabulary, including direct and indirect instruction, review, and digital tools. Similarly, chapter 7 offers strategies that are appropriate to use with English learners (ELs) and students with disabilities. At the close of each chapter, we also feature a list of digital tools applicable to the chapter's content that you can integrate into your instructional activities and independent practice. In appendix A (page 107), we provide in-depth reviews of these digital tools. They show great promise to enrich your vocabulary instruction through practice and review, and deepen independent word learning. We specifically include this resource in the hope that you will find it helpful and to provide the background you need to begin integrating digital tools and apps that support word learning into your comprehensive approach to literacy. Appendices B and C offer additional recommendations of texts that support vocabulary learning.

How You Can Use This Book to Advance Schoolwide Vocabulary

There are numerous ways you can use this book to implement a schoolwide or districtwide vocabulary framework. We suggest the following types of activities to help you move forward.

- Establish a literacy leadership team to guide and support effective vocabulary practices.
- Discuss the urgency for vocabulary instruction and the vocabulary gap that exists among many of our students.
- Engage in a faculty-wide book study to increase background knowledge and understanding of effective vocabulary instruction. Select collaborative tools to promote sharing resources and continuing engagement and conversation. Encourage other schools to do the same and engage in an online Twitter chat to share ideas. (Be sure to ask Kimberly or Angela to join in.)
- Discuss what it really means to know a word and how that impacts instruction and assessment.
- Discuss how to create a word-learning culture that supports vocabulary acquisition.
- Discuss how current vocabulary practices relate to research-based, effective instructional practices.
- Determine how to select words to support your students' academic content learning.
- Select instructional strategies suitable for elementary, secondary, and special populations.
- Integrate digital tools into word learning to practice and review general and academic vocabulary.
- Determine how to implement and support a blended vocabulary program that includes direct strategies, indirect strategies, and digital tools and games.

We provide a wealth of information and strategies in this book to support teachers, literacy teams, and professional learning communities as you discover, learn, and implement instructional strategies. However, if you begin to feel overwhelmed, keep in mind that sometimes simpler is better. You can break this process down into a few basic elements. Following are five simple steps that will help make selecting and teaching vocabulary easy yet effective as you begin to implement common schoolwide practices (Tyson, 2013c).

1. Understand the key characteristics of effective vocabulary instruction (see chapter 2).
2. Identify and sort vocabulary into the three-tiered vocabulary framework (see chapter 3).
3. Create a print-rich environment to support word learning (see chapter 4).
4. Identify and master evidence-based vocabulary strategies (see chapters 5, 6, and 7).
5. Choose digital tools that support word learning (see chapters 5, 6, and 7 and appendix A).

Recap

Vocabulary knowledge undergirds learning both in school and out. It plays a vital role both in learning to read and understanding what is read. If students don't understand the meaning of words within a novel or other text, they'll more than likely be unable to comprehend it. It is our goal, in this book, to provide you with the knowledge, skills, and dispositions to equip your students with the vocabulary they need to be successful in school and life.

Read. Think. Engage. We invite you to begin a conversation with us on social media. We always enjoy talking, tweeting, and learning with educators and literacy leaders about how to best address challenges, celebrate accomplishments, and take purposeful next steps toward literacy improvement.

NEXT STEPS

Consider the following questions individually or discuss them with colleagues or in literacy leadership team settings.

Teachers

- Do you see a large vocabulary gap among your students? What are practical steps you can take to begin addressing this gap?
- How does understanding how young children develop vocabulary impact instruction in your classroom or school? How does it impact what you share with parents?
- How would you describe the relationship between vocabulary and comprehension to a colleague? To your students?

Literacy Leadership Teams

- Think about your teaching staff. How familiar do you think your staff members are with the information we shared in this chapter?
- Discuss the vocabulary gap. Does it hold specific relevance for your student population? If so, what explicit steps can you take to address the gap? How can you support staff in doing so?
- Discuss how the staff can make certain that students who enter the school deficient in vocabulary will increase their word knowledge.
- As a team, discuss top takeaways related to the importance of vocabulary instruction. Determine big ideas that you will share with all instructional staff, including paraprofessionals and interventionists.

CHAPTER 1

A Culture of Word Learning

It seems natural to want to begin the process of fostering schoolwide vocabulary learning by digging right in and building a repertoire of effective instructional strategies. And as much as we love seeing teachers embrace research-based vocabulary strategies and integrate them into their daily instruction, the longer we work with teachers, the more we see that we need to first take a step back. Perhaps even more important than the beginning of the work around vocabulary strategies is to first create a culture of word learning—one in which everyone constantly becomes more literate. We concur with leading researchers who point to the importance of creating a schoolwide culture that supports and encourages students' ongoing learning of new words (Blachowicz et al., 2006).

While the task of addressing students' deficient vocabulary can seem overwhelming—especially in high-poverty schools—creating a culture that supports building vocabulary is a viable way to address the challenge because that's where the power of word learning begins. We've found that when teachers and leaders take the time to build the culture first and work together to create an environment that supports developing a diverse vocabulary, it sets the stage for word learning to occur throughout the entire day in every classroom. In short, vocabulary instruction becomes part of the core instruction in every subject—not just English language arts—and for every student. In this chapter, we'll examine how to develop a word-learning culture, avoid pitfalls, establish collaborative teams, address resistance to change, and select digital tools to help support collaboration and continual professional development. We'll also describe school and district literacy leadership team exemplars. In the long term, we believe that a thoughtful and diverse literacy leadership team provides the necessary foundation for creating, supporting, and sustaining a culture of word learning that will make a positive difference in the lives of your students.

Avoiding Pitfalls

Schools that enthusiastically embrace vocabulary and literacy development have typically grappled with sagging student achievement for some time. They often have a clear idea of literacy strengths and gaps based on collecting and reviewing achievement data. By targeting defined areas for improvement, they have a road map to follow. Leaders are eager to begin tackling their short- and long-term goals. However, in our work with principals and teachers, we have found that enthusiasm for word learning can sometimes actually get in the way of moving forward.

The scenario might look something like this. A principal talks with a few key teachers, makes a general announcement at the staff meeting about the new literacy initiative, and schedules several targeted professional development days focused on building a repertoire of instructional vocabulary strategies. Though well intentioned, the principal in this scenario sets up a schoolwide vocabulary initiative to become *just another initiative*. Invariably, some teachers will wait it out and count on the enthusiasm *and* the initiative to disappear eventually. Resistance has already begun. More important, with enough resisters, no *real* change will occur.

Why does this approach fail? Because it treats a literacy improvement initiative as if it's a procedural or structural change such as changing the bell times or bus schedule rather than a cultural change. Cultural changes are about transforming ways of thinking and doing. In contrast to simple procedural changes, cultural changes often meet with more resistance. However, recognizing and working toward developing a culture that supports word learning across classrooms will, in the long term, provide for continual and sustainable integration to support curricula and standards.

Developing a Literacy Leadership Team

Establishing a literacy leadership team helps ensure a strong start to provide the support teachers will need. Intentionality and planning will make a difference in whether the implementation plan will take hold and create the change necessary to reach long-term goals that result in improved student achievement. Therefore, a literacy leadership team that includes respected and influential teachers is critical.

While there is no one model of a literacy leadership team, we think that it should comprise a diverse group that includes teacher leaders from varied grade levels and content areas, an instructional or literacy coach, special education and EL teachers, a media specialist, a community outreach liaison, and a lead learner or administrator. Teams may be established in several ways. For example, team members may come from an existing school improvement team, or they may be members of a literacy or curriculum team. Establishing the team largely depends on the makeup of the school and how those groups are determined. In all cases, a diverse and inclusive team provides multiple perspectives and insights that range from how to best support teachers to reaching out to parents and community members who can also participate in the word-learning effort. As we see it, the primary purpose for the team is to communicate with, represent, and support teachers in their professional learning. The International Literacy Association's (n.d.) *Standards for Reading Professionals* provides additional information for those who wish to further define the roles and responsibilities of team members.

Regardless of a team's makeup, it is very important that members have a foundational knowledge of direct and indirect strategies for teaching vocabulary. Direct (or explicit) strategies include intentional word-learning opportunities, and indirect strategies refer to incidental word learning that can occur independently in a literacy-rich and word-conscious environment. Teachers can review and practice with integrated digital tools, apps, and games. These two main categories are a great place to begin when laying the foundation for vocabulary instruction across classrooms, so it is essential that all members have clarity on these concepts. See chapter 4 for a more in-depth discussion of these methods, and refer to chapters 5 and 6 for examples of specific applications in the classroom.

The familiar adage "Go slow to go fast" applies in the case of literacy leadership teams. Slowing down and taking the time to develop a team may seem unimportant or time consuming. However, we believe the long-term benefits are worth the effort.

Addressing Resistance

It is normal to experience resistance and pushback. Leadership teams can neutralize the negativity of those teachers who may be less than enthusiastic by discussing, planning, and establishing support structures before the real work of improved instruction begins. In the early stages, the literacy leadership team should provide the necessary expertise and leadership to support teachers as they begin implementing effective word-learning strategies.

As learning and practices deepen, team members use the principles of *tight* and *loose* leadership (DuFour & Eaker, 1998) around specific parameters for vocabulary instruction across the school. For example, they may decide that every teacher must provide direct vocabulary instruction each day in some manner (tight parameter); however, teachers determine which strategies and tools work best to support word learning for their students (loose parameter). Finally, the literacy leadership team may provide additional support and feedback to teacher teams and encourage collaboration and sharing through the use of digital tools.

Using Collaborative Tools to Support Literacy Leadership Teams

Sharing among teams and teachers is a key ingredient, we think, to keep the momentum strong across schools and is also important for continual improvement. Our term *blended vocabulary* refers not only to blending direct instruction with digital tools that extend word learning but also to blending formats of professional learning and collaboration. Teams can collaborate more simply than they once could. Traditional forms of professional learning may include sharing in staff meetings, learning from a literacy expert during a professional development day, engaging in book studies, and collaborating within a structure such as professional learning communities. While sharing and collaborating occurs during these opportunities, it can sometimes be limited to face-to-face encounters. Digital tools that support collaboration, on the other hand, allow teachers and teams to share beyond the constraints of designated times and in-person meetings, and provide a host of advantages that more traditional formats do not easily achieve. The following sections describe several effective tools and their key collaborative features. Visit **go.SolutionTree.com/literacy** for live links to these resources.

Shared Notebooks

Evernote (https://evernote.com), OneNote (www.onenote.com), and LiveBinders (www.livebinders.com) are web-based note-taking tools with sharing capabilities. Individuals create their own accounts to which they can easily add notes and notebooks. These tools have many advantages over traditional paper notebooks. Think of these tools as virtual filing cabinets. You can store various folders (called *notebooks* in these tools), each containing files (notes or pages). Useful features include the ability to easily add hyperlinks, webpages, tags, audio notes, and much more.

These virtual notebooks are perfect tools for team collaboration. Team members can easily share notebooks and pages, and no saving is necessary—changes to notebooks and pages save and sync automatically. As teachers learn and explore vocabulary strategies, they can easily share websites, tools, lesson plans, word lists, and more.

Twitter

Teams can take advantage of online collaborative tools such as Twitter (https://twitter.com) to share ideas and celebrations along the journey. For example, we encourage teams to create a Twitter hashtag (#) using the name or initials of the school district, such as #Waynevocab or #ZSDvocab, to aggregate tweets from teachers. Across your school or district, teachers can tweet hyperlinks to strategies, vocabulary games, and digital tools. Additionally, they can tweet images of word walls and photos that show how they are integrating vocabulary learning across classrooms, schools, and the district.

Another way the leadership team can use this social media is to host a Twitter chat at a designated time. Leaders can use a hashtag such as #vocabchat to aggregate tweets, and facilitate the chat by posting questions such as, What is your number-one go-to vocabulary strategy for EL students? Participants introduce themselves at the beginning of the session and tweet responses to questions, including the hashtag #vocabchat following each response. Leaders can also invite vocabulary experts such as Kimberly or Angela to share insights, collaborate, and provide feedback to the instructional community. (Be sure to use the hashtag #blendedvocab to join in our ongoing discussion of this book and its concepts on Twitter.) If you are new to Twitter, we recommend downloading the popular *Twitter Cheat Sheet* (Tyson, 2012e) that helps teachers get up to speed quickly.

Backchannels

Backchannels are another popular way to collaborate, share thoughts and links, and receive feedback during professional learning. Think of backchannels as a means for participants to have background conversations that take place at the same time as the professional development session. Teachers can ask the presenter or other participants a question during the session without interrupting the flow of the session. Within the backchannel, participants can also easily share links, as they think of them during the presentation, to websites that may benefit other participants. There are several websites you can use for backchanneling. TodaysMeet (www.todaysmeet.com) is free and easy to use, and it's the one that we have used most frequently at conferences. Other similar sites include Chatzy (www.chatzy.com) and Backchannel Chat (www.backchannelchat .com). We encourage you to learn more about backchannels by viewing the YouTube video *Todays Meet for Classroom Backchannels* (Brent @ EdTech.tv, 2015) and setting up your own backchannel to support professional learning.

Pinterest

Pinterest (www.pinterest.com) is a social curation network that allows users to share and categorize images. Users "pin" images, videos, and other visual information to categorized boards. Users can browse and discover what other users have pinned as well. In its simplest form, Pinterest is a huge, online bulletin board. Teachers could save and share ideas about word walls and vocabulary strategies on the site to support implementing vocabulary across grade levels and content areas.

Wikis

Wikis are websites that allow all users to create, edit, and alter information; how it's presented; and how it's structured. A school or a system could create a wiki as a storage and collaborative space for instructional strategies, templates, and bulletin board ideas, all with the intent of improving vocabulary instruction.

Google Docs and Google Sites

Many teachers use Google Docs to create, edit, and collaborate among colleagues. While sharing and collaborating with Google Docs is simple, educators can quickly and easily set up a Google Site to support vocabulary implementation. The site can serve as a common place for embedding documents, lesson plans, presentations, videos, links to websites, and more.

Examining Literacy Leadership Team Exemplars

In the following sections, we provide examples of both a schoolwide literacy leadership team and a districtwide literacy leadership team we've worked with, detailing how they worked together and the success they were able to achieve.

Schoolwide Literacy Leadership Teams

A large, urban elementary school that Kimberly supported found that its literacy leadership team made all the difference in making word learning stick across the school. Garden City Elementary School, serving a culturally diverse and high-poverty student population in Indianapolis, created a team representing many grade levels and varied teaching and nonteaching positions to guide its vocabulary instruction efforts.

Through the team's leadership, teachers created a common language and understanding of the importance of vocabulary acquisition and created a culture that supported word learning across the school day. With an all-in attitude, teachers and staff encouraged word learning in and out of classrooms. Word walls and bulletin boards featuring vocabulary were displayed across classrooms and peppered in hallways, the cafeteria, and the gymnasium. Partnering with school leadership, the team provided support to teachers and grade-level collaborative teams. They established expectations for vocabulary by targeting vocabulary strategies, modeling those strategies for teachers, and monitoring implementation across classrooms. They also encouraged teachers as they integrated vocabulary into their daily lessons and identified words to teach. By supporting *and* modeling, Garden City teachers were able to sustain their emphasis on schoolwide vocabulary development over five years, raising student achievement in the process. Additionally, the school's state report card grade went from D to A during this time. Staff members continue to focus on vocabulary across classrooms and share their successes with their community and educators worldwide using the Twitter hashtag #WeAreWayne.

Districtwide Literacy Leadership Teams

In a midsize suburban district, vocabulary development was an integral part of an overall literacy implementation plan. This district tackled leadership in a more comprehensive manner—one that fit their needs and goals. In order to move vocabulary learning forward districtwide, district leaders developed literacy leadership teams at every school. In addition, they established a districtwide literacy implementation team made up of three or four members from each schoolwide team, a principal or assistant principal, media center specialists, and central office leaders.

The districtwide team met monthly for intensive professional development in a train-the-trainer fashion. During this time, the schoolwide teams unpacked the *what*, *why*, and *how* necessary for creating a culture and structures that support integrating word learning across schools. They learned how to implement a wide repertoire of both direct and indirect instructional strategies. Additionally, based on their data, they established districtwide goals as well as individual schoolwide goals.

This approach allowed schools to work on individual schoolwide goals while keeping district targets in mind. Teams were accountable to share progress and strategies both within schools and districtwide. Each time the districtwide team met, members of school teams shared their targeted schoolwide strategies, specific goals, and progress toward achieving those goals. In this case, having both schoolwide and districtwide teams kept momentum going across the many moving parts associated with large-scale implementation. Intentionally aligning the system and building goals is almost always a precursor to increased achievement in any content area, and so it is in this case.

Recap

Vocabulary work is vital in our students' lives. To ensure you implement vocabulary instruction well, it's important to take the time to step back, perhaps before you begin the work, to think about developing a culture that supports word learning, establishing collaborative teams, and selecting digital tools that will help sustain your work. Creating a school- or districtwide culture that generates word consciousness, provides professional learning opportunities, and uses digital tools that support collaboration as teachers implement a blended vocabulary approach is an ambitious but worthwhile goal. We suggest that schools and districts resist the urge to jump into learning instructional strategies, and instead, begin by developing literacy leadership teams that can provide the support, modeling, feedback, and collaboration necessary to create systematic and sustainable vocabulary improvement. In the long term, we believe that a thoughtful and diverse literacy leadership team provides the necessary foundation for creating, supporting, and sustaining a culture of word learning that will make a positive difference in the lives of your students.

Digital Tools for Literacy Leadership Team Collaboration

Backchannel Chat (www.backchannelchat.com): Backchannel site
Chatzy (www.chatzy.com): Backchannel site
Evernote (https://evernote.com): Digital notebook
LiveBinders (www.livebinders.com): Digital notebook
OneNote (www.onenote.com): Digital notebook
TodaysMeet (www.todaysmeet.com): Backchannel site
Twitter (https://twitter.com): Social media

NEXT STEPS

Consider the following questions individually or discuss them with colleagues or in literacy leadership team settings.

Teachers

- Do you think your school culture values and supports word learning? What could you do to encourage colleagues to promote word acquisition and word consciousness?
- How could you convince coworkers who teach nonacademic subjects or serve in another capacity in the school to become more active in teaching vocabulary?
- Think about direct and indirect instructional strategies you currently use in the classroom. How could you improve the use of indirect means to promote word consciousness?
- Which digital tools are you most interested in learning how to use to collaborate and share with colleagues?

- If you're not familiar with Evernote and OneNote, consider learning more about their flexibility and utility to capture notes and websites. Try sharing a notebook with a colleague for collaboration and further learning.

Literacy Leadership Teams

- Gain a general idea of where your school is with vocabulary development. Discuss this with your grade-level teams, academic leadership team, collaborative teams, or building leadership team.
- Think about who you should include in a schoolwide literacy leadership team in your building. Why did you include each individual? How about in your district?
- As a team, discuss an initiative currently underway in your school and district. How does vocabulary align with this initiative? How can you help colleagues see that this is not just one more thing added to the plate?
- How could your team provide ongoing professional learning specific to vocabulary? Consider who would provide the training and what resources (time and financial) you have for training and ongoing support.
- Do you see teachers and staff using indirect opportunities to encourage word learning? If not, why not? If so, what strategies do they most commonly use?
- How can the literacy leadership team support incidental word learning across the school? What about across the entire system?
- Do you currently use digital tools that support collaboration and professional learning? Which tools do you think would best support sharing and collaborating among teachers in your school or across the district?
- Consider using digital tools for collaborating and creating a Twitter hashtag for your school or district to promote collaboration around word learning. Consider hosting a Twitter chat to foster deeper discussion of frameworks, content, and strategies.
- Become familiar with a backchannel such as TodaysMeet, and begin incorporating it into a professional development session to encourage collaboration and sharing during the learning session.
- Think about creating a shared vocabulary notebook in Evernote or OneNote. Grade-level or academic teams may wish to create their own notebooks and collaborate within them. Invite teachers to add lesson plans, videos, websites, and more to the notebook. The YouTube video *Evernote Tips: The 11 Amazing Features That Make Using Evernote So Freaking Awesome* (Evernote Scott, 2012) provides great tips for new users. *Microsoft OneNote Tutorial* (Cox, 2014) will similarly get teams up to speed with OneNote. Visit **go.SolutionTree.com/literacy** for live links to these resources.
- What digital tools described here do you currently use? Which tools do you think would best support sharing and collaborating among teachers in your school or across the district?

CHAPTER 2

A New Model for Effective Vocabulary Instruction

Many esteemed educators and researchers have proposed models for (or components of) an effective vocabulary program. While instructional strategies are important, models allow educators to think conceptually about what components they must include in a comprehensive approach to vocabulary. This chapter summarizes some of the most widely used models and proposes a new one we have synthesized from them, combined with areas of need that we have seen in school settings.

A Review of Existing Models

Before we propose our blended model, we first want to share some background information on three extant models from which we have drawn various aspects. We'll highlight the benefits and some of the struggles we've seen educators encounter in their use of these models.

Marzano's Six-Step Model

Robert J. Marzano (2004) recommends a six-step process for teaching vocabulary in his book *Building Background Knowledge for Academic Achievement.* The steps are as follows.

1. The teacher provides a description, explanation, or example of the new term.
2. Students provide a linguistic explanation by restating the new term in their own words using an example, description, or explanation of the term.
3. Students create a nonlinguistic representation of the term, which may include constructing a picture, pictograph, or symbolic representation, or acting out the term.
4. Over time, students periodically engage in activities that help them deepen their knowledge of the vocabulary term while recording those terms in a print or online vocabulary notebook.
5. Periodically, teachers ask students to discuss terms with one another.
6. Students, over time, engage in game-like activities that allow them to play with the terms and reinforce word knowledge.

In our work with teachers, we've frequently helped them embed this framework as a regular part of a schoolwide approach to vocabulary. This set of steps appeals to both teachers and students. For example, embedded within the model are recursive learning and multiple exposures to words, fundamental factors in effective word learning. The model also puts students in charge of their own word learning by having them develop nonlinguistic representations of words, maintain word journals, and play with words.

Step 1 begins the process with direct instruction, in which teachers use student-friendly definitions. Steps 2 and 3 allow students to start making the words their own through both linguistic and nonlinguistic representations. The remaining three steps provide for using and reviewing the words over time, engaging in varied activities with words, including games, and authentic application of the words. The steps unfold over time, making learning new words a seamless and recurring part of the learning process in any discipline. In sum, this framework has many positive aspects, and we know teachers who embrace it enthusiastically.

We have worked with teachers who earnestly seek to implement the entire framework with fidelity. However, some teachers find they tend to put steps 4, 5, and 6 on the back burner or don't get to them as frequently as they do steps 1, 2, and 3. Other teachers mistakenly think they should do all six steps when teaching specific new vocabulary words instead of teaching words over time. Also, teachers often express confusion about how many words they can teach at a time with the six steps. They feel that they may spend far too much time on only a few words versus teaching a larger number of words, perhaps more superficially. As we try to convey throughout this book, we think effective vocabulary instruction has a great deal to do with intentionality and purpose. In chapter 3, we'll unpack how to select words for in-depth instruction. Although the framework is useful for teaching some words in depth, keep in mind that not all words need a six-step approach.

Graves's Model

Michael Graves's work focuses tightly on literacy in general and on vocabulary in particular. His work is well respected in literacy circles, and other vocabulary researchers almost always reference it in publications. Graves (2006) proposes a solid four-part model for vocabulary instruction, which we briefly outline here.

1. **Provide rich and varied language experiences:** This includes students experiencing words through reading, listening, speaking, and writing across grade levels, content areas, and genres. Reading aloud to students and providing time for them to read materials of choice are an important part of this component.
2. **Teach individual words:** This element focuses on teaching new words explicitly. Teachers may use various instructional strategies during this planned instruction, including nonlinguistic representations and cooperative learning.
3. **Teach word-learning strategies:** This component includes teaching word analysis strategies, inference strategies, and the effective use of resources such as print and online dictionaries.

4. **Foster word consciousness:** Create an environment rich in print and language opportunities that engage students in playful activities with words, and serve as an exemplar of good vocabulary use.

In contrast to Marzano's model, the first part of Graves's model provides for many indirect means of learning words, whereas Marzano's approach is more of a direct instruction model. Marzano does not address read-alouds, independent reading, or word consciousness in his model. These exclusions do not mean, however, that Marzano doesn't think incidental word learning builds vocabulary; he includes incidental word learning from reading in all of his publications about vocabulary. In his six-step model, he simply focuses on the transition from direct instruction to guided practice to independent word learning and practice and leaves most of the recommendations about reading to other researchers.

The second part of Graves's model aligns most directly with Marzano's entire six-step cycle. It is important to note, however, that Marzano specifically calls for both nonlinguistic representations of words and cooperative learning throughout steps 3 through 6. You probably recognize from the comparison thus far that the Graves recommendations are more comprehensive.

The third part of Graves's model has been a crucial part of the vocabulary instruction many of us received in school and of the instruction we've provided, especially if we have been English language arts or reading teachers. Studying word parts like roots and affixes, making inferences from context within the selection, and using glossaries and dictionaries are all important vocabulary expansion strategies. However, they often receive too much time and emphasis in classrooms—to the detriment of the other areas to which Graves calls our attention. In addition, word-learning strategies can easily become workbook or worksheet focused and disconnected from integrated vocabulary instruction.

The fourth part of the model, fostering word consciousness, is one that educators often overlook or relegate to a status of "if we get around to that," and it's a shame. All adults in a school building can serve as wonderful models of word use, and they can also continually show interest in and enthusiasm for word learning. A teacher who is endlessly curious about words creates students who are curious about—and not afraid of—words.

Beck's Model

Third, Isabel Beck and colleagues (2013), whose work is cited in appendix A of the Common Core State Standards for English language arts (NGA & CCSSO, n.d.), recommend the following five steps in what they call *robust vocabulary instruction.*

1. **Contextualize words:** Put simply, this means presenting new words in context, not in lists. Students should study words in the context in which texts present them.
2. **Provide friendly explanations:** These employ general terms that students can readily understand, not gobbledygook dictionary definitions. We often call these *student-friendly definitions.* Teachers can reference the dictionary definition, but it is not the focal point of this step.

3. **Provide another context for the word:** Make sure students know that the context in which they found the word may not be the only context in which they can use it. Providing varied contexts helps students connect to the word.

4. **Provide opportunities for students to actively process word meanings:** Have them connect the known to the unknown. Ask questions that use more than one target word at a time to help students see relationships and contrasts between words. Providing similar and contrasting relationships (using, for example, language such as *is like* and *isn't like*) between words is quite helpful for students to move word knowledge from unknown to known.

5. **Provide many encounters with the words over time:** Revisiting words and providing multiple exposures are paramount in word learning. Encounters need to include multiple applications of the words, meaning that students use the words in different contexts, different ways, and so on. The more the words pop up in the students' reading, writing, speaking, listening, and viewing, the more likely students are to remember them.

Beck's step 5, encounters over time, connects directly to Marzano's steps 4, 5, and 6. Additionally, Beck's step 4 mirrors the second part of Graves's model.

These three models overlap significantly, and we can glean much good advice from them. We have certainly returned to their ideas over and over for guidance and inspiration in our own teaching careers. However, we feel that teachers, as part of the learning communities they represent, should take the best from what others have researched and proposed, consider the model we describe in the following section, and devise instruction that will work best for them and their students.

The Blended Vocabulary Model

We propose a new, three-dimensional model to represent a comprehensive approach to vocabulary learning. It is a flexible model that brings together the best aspects of several existing structures, including those from Marzano, Graves, and Beck. Distinct advantages include allowing for many effective strategies within its structure, the ability for teachers to add past successful lessons to the model, and the easy applicability of its components to a schoolwide or districtwide vocabulary effort.

Briefly, our model consists of three parts. Why only three? Because three is concise (and precise) enough for busy teachers to keep in mind as they provide instruction in all the concepts and topics they teach on any given day. Three also implies a sense of balance, like a three-legged stool. With three components, it's difficult for one component to greatly overshadow or outweigh the others. The components we recommend include the following.

1. **Modeling:** Model robust vocabulary and interest in words. All adults with whom students interact during the school day should do this.

2. **Explicit instruction:** Teach students targeted words and proven word-learning strategies so they can tackle learning words on their own. Use digital tools as part of instruction, review, and practice.

3. **Incidental learning:** Provide for incidental vocabulary learning. Acquiring vocabulary through incidental experience occurs through a print-rich environment and various literacy experiences, including read-alouds, independent reading, and school and community events like dramatic performances, family literacy nights, and poetry slams, to name just a few. Setting up experiences such as these provides the backdrop and support for student-led, incidental word learning.

See figure 2.1 for an illustration of how the model functions.

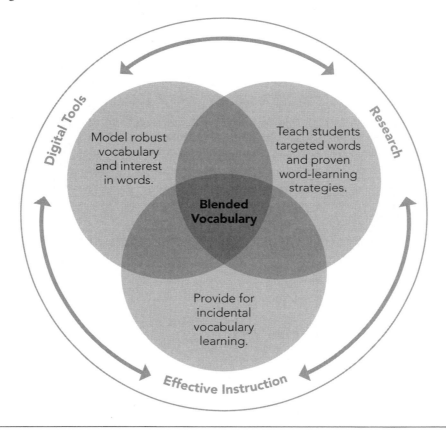

Figure 2.1: The blended vocabulary model.

As noted previously in this chapter, this model draws from key aspects of the Marzano (2004), Beck et al. (2013), and Graves (2006) models, which also overlap and align in multiple ways. See table 2.1 (page 22) for a quick reference and comparison of the key aspects of each of these models and our blended model.

Modeling

Part 1, modeling, calls attention to what many excellent teachers of vocabulary do almost seamlessly. These teachers speak to students in ways that other teachers may not. For example, Angela once knew a teacher who would use all sorts of synonyms for basic or overused words with her students. If she needed a student to take the attendance

Table 2.1: A Comparison of Four Vocabulary Models

Marzano's Model	Beck's Model	Graves's Model	Blended Vocabulary Model
1. The teacher provides a description, explanation, or example of the new term.	1. Contextualize words.	1. Provide rich and varied language experiences.	1. Model robust vocabulary and interest in words.
2. Students provide a linguistic explanation by restating the new term in their own words using an example, description, or explanation of the term.	2. Provide friendly explanations.	2. Teach individual words.	2. Teach students targeted words and proven word-learning strategies so they can tackle learning words on their own.
3. Students create a nonlinguistic representation of the term, which may include a picture, pictograph, symbolic representation, or acting out the term.	3. Provide another context for the word.	3. Teach word-learning strategies.	3. Provide for incidental vocabulary learning.
4. Over time, students periodically engage in activities that help them deepen their understanding and record terms in a print or online vocabulary notebook.	4. Provide opportunities for students to actively process word meanings.	4. Foster word consciousness.	
5. Periodically, students discuss terms with one another.	5. Provide many encounters with words over time.		
6. Students, over time, engage in game-like activities that allow them to play with the terms and reinforce word knowledge.			

information or some other document to the office, she might say something like, "Jackson, please ambulate to the main office and deliver this for me," or "Please convey this document to the authority who is noted at the top." She strived to use unfamiliar and sometimes far more sophisticated words to replace words like *walk*, *go*, *take*, *say*, *good*, and *nice*. Because she often accompanied unfamiliar words with a known task or exaggerated gestures, her students quickly grasped a basic definition. They enjoyed figuring out what she was saying, and many of them also delighted in using the terms they had learned in their other classes. Other teachers were impressed that these students, many of whom struggled mightily in reading and writing, learned useful, rich words through such indirect means. This is a great example of an intentional, embedded method of promoting rich word learning.

Another part of modeling is attending to unusual or unknown words when they appear in text a class is reading aloud, in a video they are viewing, or in announcements coming over the loudspeaker—anywhere students see and hear words. That's where teachers can find an opportunity to model enthusiasm about words and, if the moment is right, provide students with a quick synonym or summary for a word so that they can begin to understand it, at the least, on a surface level. In the current climate of demanding standards, abundant content, and countless hours of testing, teachers often say they don't have enough time to teach. Remembering to be a good model of word learning takes very little extra time during the day. Instead, it's an integrated approach to excite enthusiasm for word learning that can go far in enhancing literacy learning for our students.

This portion of our model aligns most closely with Beck's advice about providing many encounters with words over time. Teachers who remember to use certain synonyms for words like *walk* and *talk*, for example, will support their students in using the same more precise and less common words. This segment of our model also follows Graves's suggestion to foster word consciousness. Teachers are, in our opinion, perhaps the best models of being interested in and delighted by words.

Explicit Instruction

The second part of the model involves explicit instruction, including the support of digital tools. Explicit instruction is obvious in Marzano's model beginning with (and perhaps appearing most prominently in) the first step, where the teacher provides a description, explanation, or example of the new term. Graves urges teachers to teach both specific words and word-learning strategies, which are encompassed in our model. And lastly, Beck's steps focus squarely on explicit instruction as they direct teachers to contextualize words, provide student-friendly definitions, and provide additional contexts.

As Marzano (2004), Graves (2006), Beck et al. (2013), and others cited in this book have noted, explicit vocabulary instruction is rare in U.S. schools. With the development and publication of the Common Core State Standards—and with the resulting political backlash against them—one thing is certain: the CCSS have come under intense scrutiny. This focus has helped draw attention to vocabulary acquisition and use like no other standards document in history. Teachers everywhere (and many parents) now know about Isabel Beck's three-tiered framework of classifying words. Because Beck's classification system is now widely known, it follows that educators now ask themselves, "Which words should I spend the most time and energy explicitly teaching?"

As we conducted research for this book by scouring academic journals, online sources, and published professional books on vocabulary learning, we noted that references to digital tools and their impact on literacy learning are somewhat sparse (though they are growing). While we may lack direct research on many of these tools, we have observed firsthand the positive impact they make in teachers' explicit instruction and students' engagement. Classroom researchers continue to supply empirical evidence to provide implications and support for integrating digital tools into direct instructional activities and independent practice (Hutchison & Colwell, 2014).

While we have some advice in chapter 3 about how to select words wisely, this part of the framework is about providing effective direct instruction. It includes teaching specific words—choose these wisely based on the standard, the task, and various other factors—and strategies to employ with unfamiliar words. It also includes teaching word parts and morphology so that students understand how to unlock unknown words when they encounter them. Students also need to learn how to use context, particularly in informational text, to help them determine meaning.

For teachers who are not readily familiar with or comfortable with technology, the task of selecting appropriate tools to support these learning goals can seem daunting. There are many ways to become familiar with online tools and, perhaps of greater interest, to learn how other educators select digital tools to use and for what purposes. The following tips and resources will help you begin developing your own curated selection of digital tools to best serve you and your students. Visit **go.SolutionTree.com/literacy** for live links to these resources. See appendix A (page 107) for extensive descriptions and reviews of some tools we find especially useful. However, keep in mind that existing online tools may evolve and disappear over time, and new tools will emerge. Knowing how to find and evaluate new and evolved tools will enable you to continue using the most effective, current, and relevant tools available, regardless of these inevitable changes. Consulting the following resources will enable you to do just that.

Education Organization Websites

To begin, we suggest following several popular educational organizations and individual educator blogs that frequently provide recommendations and reviews of online tools and apps. Some of our favorite groups and organizations include the following.

- TeachThought (www.teachthought.com)
- Edutopia (www.edutopia.org)
- Edudemic (www.edudemic.com)
- International Society for Technology in Education (ISTE; www.iste.org)

Blogs

Individual blogs we follow include Vicki Davis's *CoolCatTeacher* (www.coolcat teacher. com) and *Mr. Nussbaum* (www.mrnussbaum.com), written by a classroom teacher who provides comprehensive reviews of games and apps. Kimberly also frequently blogs specifically about digital tools and apps that support literacy and vocabulary at *Dr. Kimberly's Literacy Blog* (www.kimberlytyson.com).

Social Media

In addition to blogs, many teachers use Twitter and Pinterest to find recommendations, reviews, and classroom solutions (often referred to as *hacks*). If you're not familiar with either of these social media outlets, you can download Kimberly's popular cheat sheets for Twitter (Tyson, 2012e) and Pinterest (Tyson, 2012d) and get up to speed in no time. Those already active on Twitter can still learn new ideas and tools by joining a Twitter chat group such as #web20tools, #sigetc, or #iPadchat. Each of these groups has weekly or biweekly chats specifically about technology and shares ideas for using digital tools in the classroom. If you're a Twitter newbie, you can check out many educator chat groups and the times they meet using Kimberly's *Cheat Sheet: 101+ Twitter Chat Groups for Educators {12 Days of Literacy}* (Tyson, 2013d). You'll find simple steps outlining how to join a chat group, follow hashtags, and contribute to the online conversation.

These resources as well as others will help set you on the path to selecting digital tools that support your curricular goals. For those teachers who are new to integrating technology, the Technology Integration Planning Cycle for Literacy and Language Arts (Hutchison & Woodward, 2014) may be a useful planning tool to navigate selecting digital tools and aligning them to instructional goals. Choose which resources work best for you as you discover more about digital tools that support a comprehensive approach to vocabulary expansion.

Incidental Learning

The third part of the model is about doing all you can to encourage incidental learning of words. We know that students will never learn enough words from direct instruction and modeling alone to adequately address the vocabulary gap. As educators, we must intentionally build word consciousness in a variety of ways. Students also need to learn words incidentally within a print-rich environment that supports and encourages word learning. Incidental word learning includes opportunities to engage in independent reading, listening to peers use interesting words, and engaging in games and playful activity. The best incidental word learning occurs in a robust, literate environment across classrooms where print and ebooks, newspapers, word walls, labels, anchor charts, and posters provide rich context and exposure to words.

We also encourage schools to ensure that students are able to attend dramatic performances, host events like poetry slams at coffeehouses where both students and community artists can interact, and hold family literacy nights that surround everyone with words in a pleasurable context. For example, several elementary schools in Kokomo School District in Indiana host popular vocabulary parades each year where students dress up in costumes ranging from simple to outrageous—each representing a vocabulary word. This fun, engaging idea, which reinforces nonlinguistic word learning, originates from the book *Miss Alaineus: A Vocabulary Disaster* by Debra Frasier (2000).

Incidental word learning, the third element of the blended vocabulary model, aligns with the three previously mentioned models of word learning. For example, it aligns with

Marzano's model when he suggests using games that enable students to play with words and be exposed to unfamiliar words while engaging in game-like activities. Beck suggests providing many encounters with words over time, which includes reviewing words and developing word awareness through read-alouds, print, and conversation. Graves's model directly aligns with providing incidental word-learning opportunities when he suggests providing rich and varied language experience and building word consciousness through direct and indirect activities.

The powerful vocabulary and constant enthusiasm that the teacher models, the explicit instruction the teacher provides, and the time and structures the teacher creates for incidental vocabulary learning all combine to form a model that is well defined and research based yet adaptable to unique situations.

Recap

Models for teaching vocabulary are a viable component of a schoolwide or districtwide framework for teaching vocabulary. They help educators develop a common language and understanding around essential or core components of effective vocabulary instruction. In this chapter, we've reviewed three valuable models for vocabulary instruction and proposed a new, three-part model suitable for guiding effective direct and indirect word-learning opportunities to help students build broad, rich vocabularies.

NEXT STEPS

Consider the following questions individually or discuss them with colleagues or in literacy leadership team settings.

Teachers
- Review the frameworks for vocabulary instruction in this chapter. Were you already familiar with any of them?
- Do you see any advantages or disadvantages of aligning with a specific model for vocabulary instruction? Why or why not?
- What component or components of the models are most important to you?
- What resonates with you regarding the three-part blended vocabulary model? How does this model align with your current vocabulary instruction?

Literacy Leadership Teams
- Do you think aligning your school with a model for vocabulary instruction is important? Why or why not?
- Look closely at the chart summarizing the four models for vocabulary instruction (table 2.1, page 22). Discuss similarities and differences as outlined within this chapter. Which model aligns best with your schoolwide goals? Why?
- How could you present a model or models to teaching staff and allow time for discussion?

- The blended vocabulary model provides a new way of thinking about vocabulary instruction by integrating digital tools to support practice and review. How does this model support your goals for word learning?
- Discuss how the literacy leadership team can support teachers as they implement instructional strategies that align with one of the models to support schoolwide vocabulary development.
- Consider creating a shared Google Doc or wiki or hosting a Twitter chat to encourage discussion and go deeper into frameworks, content, and strategies.

CHAPTER 3

Methods for Classifying and Selecting Vocabulary Words

As we discussed previously, many students enter our classrooms with limited vocabulary knowledge. That deficiency motivates teachers to select specific vocabulary to deliberately and routinely teach and assess within lessons. While the task of teaching vocabulary is important, it can sometimes feel daunting. So many words! So little time! How do you choose? In this chapter, we'll break down this task into something less overwhelming and more manageable. Because selecting words for study is a crucial initial step in designing effective instruction, we'll begin this chapter with a discussion of the tiered vocabulary structure and its pertinent implications. Then, we'll share several different categories for classifying vocabulary words that will help teachers navigate their options and choose words based on their lesson objectives.

Understanding Tiered Vocabulary

Tiered vocabulary is an organizational structure for categorizing words into three levels and has implications for identifying the academic vocabulary that might be most useful for your students. Isabel L. Beck, Margaret G. McKeown, and Linda Kucan (2013) developed the structure and published it in their seminal work *Bringing Words to Life: Robust Vocabulary Instruction*.

We've been using the three-tiered framework with teachers for years, and many find it easy to understand and use when selecting words for instruction. However, the three tiers have garnered increased attention in the past few years because appendix A of the CCSS (NGA & CCSSO, n.d.) includes an explanation of them. Teachers now strive to understand the tiers at a deeper level than ever before. Tier one consists of basic, everyday words that are a part of most students' vocabulary. We use these words every day in conversation, and learn most of them by hearing family, peers, and teachers use them when speaking. Sometimes referred to as a student's *walking around*—or *everyday*—vocabulary, this tier includes the words a person needs to know in order to accomplish normal, everyday tasks and communicate at a basic, necessary level. Some examples include the words *big*, *small*, *up*, *down*, *house*, *family*, *table*, *smile*, *talk*, *eat*, and *sleep*.

Most native speakers know tier one words, which are generally not the focus of direct instruction. Students acquire these words naturally and over time through oral language. However, it is important to keep in mind that English learners may not be familiar with them. If your school or classroom includes students who are learning or have recently become proficient in the English language, then tier one words must be part of their vocabulary instruction. In addition, labeling items in the environment and creating word walls can support students as they acquire these critical tier one words. The information we provide throughout the rest of this chapter largely applies to native English speakers. See chapter 7 for a deeper discussion of instruction as it applies to English learners.

Tier two words include frequently occurring words that play an important role in verbal functioning across a variety of content areas. These are general academic words with high utility across a wide range of topics and contexts. Words like *justify*, *explain*, *predict*, *summarize*, *infer*, *generalize*, *conclusion*, *revolution*, and *reflection* fall into tier two. Another way to think of tier two vocabulary is as cross-curricular terms. For example, the terms *justify* and *predict* frequently appear in science, social studies, and English texts.

Going a little deeper, tier two contains words that appear in various contexts and across many topics. For example, a *reflection* can be a cognitive concept (something a character in a story is doing), a reflection of light in science, or a flip over a line in mathematics. Tier two words appear both in print and in oral language in many disciplines. Thus, teaching tier two vocabulary helps students acquire and master a wide range of words that they will encounter in many contexts.

Students learn tier two words primarily through reading and explicit instruction, in contrast to tier one words, which they generally learn through oral language. Tier two words are important in that they build a strong academic vocabulary that is key to comprehending information in many forms, especially in academic, nonfiction text. Because academic words such as *justify*, *expand*, *maximum*, and *barren* are found in many content-area texts, such as social studies, science, mathematics, English, and history texts, teachers should devote time and attention to them. Creating a streamlined list of words helps teachers focus their instructional efforts and use strategies that help students understand the nuances associated with these words in varied settings in order to master them. See appendix B (page 121) for a list of texts containing suggested tier two vocabulary words for primary and intermediate grades.

Tier three words are low-frequency, specialized, academic words. Beck and her colleagues (2008, 2013) use the term *domain-specific* to describe them, with the word *domain* referring to a specific discipline. These are terms like *isotope*, *carcinogens*, *photosynthesis*, *onomatopoeia*, *stanza*, *rhombus*, *quadratic formula*, *sarcophagus*, *hegemony*, *a cappella*, and *chiaroscuro*. These words are highly specific and not widely generalizable (if at all). Texts do not use them in multiple ways or in various contexts. We can expect that students are unfamiliar with these words.

See figure 3.1 for an illustration of how these tiers function. Using tiered vocabulary doesn't have to be complicated. With a basic understanding of the three tiers, educators can develop a framework to help select vocabulary for direct instruction.

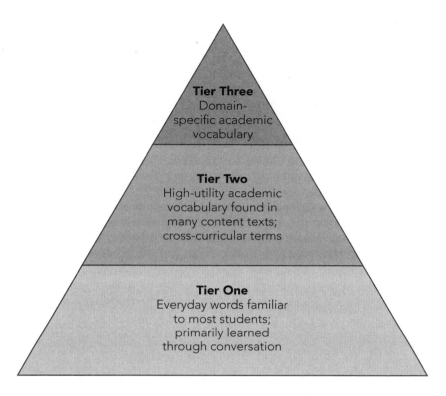

Source: Tyson, 2013f.

Figure 3.1: Tiered vocabulary.

In this chapter, we emphasize defining and recognizing the three tiers because they create an important framework for selecting and teaching words. Well-intentioned teachers often focus primarily on teaching and assessing tier three words, since they aid in comprehending specific content. Although we anticipate that students will be unfamiliar with tier three words, Beck and McKeown (1985) suggest teaching these words as the need arises for comprehension in content areas. In other words, frontload tier three terms before a lesson and prior to when students read text or other materials; however, don't allow tier three vocabulary to become the sole focus of word learning. Tier two words should consume most of our teaching time, while we should include selected tier three words, roots, and affixes as part of a comprehensive vocabulary program (Tyson, 2013f).

We suggest spending some time discussing identification and selection of tiered vocabulary. To that end, we offer the reproducible tool "Sorting Vocabulary Words Into Tiers" at the end of this chapter (page 36), designed to help teachers go deeper in this framework and practice sorting vocabulary words by tiers.

Selecting Vocabulary

Selecting words is critically important within a schoolwide effort to improve literacy. Like many instructional tasks, the decisions related to selecting vocabulary are on a continuum of choices and are largely dependent on your goals and desired learning outcomes. While the Common Core State Standards place a premium on vocabulary, they do not mention *how* to select words. With a few key ideas and strategies, teachers can make more intentional choices when selecting words and feel more confident about those selections. We provide suggestions for types and sources of words you may select to create targeted lists that support and extend content-area texts and literature, and for how to develop districtwide vocabulary lists that span content and standards. We also note the likely tiers these types of words may encompass and recommend resources that identify words in these categories.

General Knowledge Words

These lists of words are perhaps the easiest to develop. Think about your classroom, content area, grade level, and school. Perhaps begin by brainstorming specific words that you commonly use and that are necessary for students to function well within your classroom as well as in the schoolwide community. In addition, many lists available on the Internet include general words English learners should know. These lists are a great place to begin as teachers develop general knowledge word lists. One of the most popular lists is Edward Fry's (2000) *instant words*, which also appear on an abundance of websites and professional resources. Another is the Dolch (1948) list of sight words, also available online and in print. We encourage you and your colleagues to consult these lists if you need support with brainstorming tier one words that are most applicable to your students.

Academic Vocabulary

Whether teaching about single-digit addition or the quadratic formula, teachers must tackle and define academic vocabulary. To begin, teachers should select a unit of study for which to create key vocabulary lists, placing a manageable boundary on the task. We suggest the following simple sequence of steps. First, teachers review key terms and separate them into already-known words (tier one), must-know words (tier two), and should-know words (tier three). Tier two and tier three words then become the focus of instruction. One word of caution here: we find that teachers often overestimate the number of must-know words. Be sure that the words you identify for this level are truly the ones students must know in order to understand the key content.

At the elementary level, we suggest that grade-level teams develop content word lists with teachers of varied grade levels to ensure *vertical alignment* (aligning vertically through the grade levels, as opposed to horizontally, which is across one grade level). For example, third-grade teachers should compare their mathematics vocabulary with teachers in grades 2 and 4 in order to align their lists across grades without too much overlap. This will also help reveal must-know words in one grade because teams will consider already-known words at the next grade level, and vice versa (for example, an already-known word at grade 4 would most likely be a must-know word at grade 3). The vertical articulation piece is critical so that, to follow this example, fourth graders don't end up unfamiliar with important content words they should have learned in grades 2 and 3, making them deficient in specific content knowledge.

For secondary teachers, we suggest that academic departments compare lists for tier two vocabulary across content subjects and expand students' general vocabulary knowledge. An excellent resource for general academic vocabulary is Robert J. Marzano and Julia A. Simms's (2013) book *Vocabulary for the Common Core*.

Words That Appear in State Standards

In *Teaching the Critical Vocabulary of the Common Core*, Marilee Sprenger (2013) identifies fifty-five words that make or break student understanding, including specific words that appear in standards beginning in the lower grades and continuing through the higher-level grades. Most fit under the category of tier two words and include nouns and verbs, with a few adjectives and adverbs in the mix. While this list is specific to the Common Core State Standards, the idea of selecting tier two words from your state standards in a similar fashion is worthy. This resource serves as a solid starting point for teachers as they identify words from state standards.

Districtwide K–12 Core Vocabulary Lists

Tier two words are important for students to master and understand deeply, which means they can apply these words appropriately when speaking, listening, reading, and writing. Many districts we work with create K–12 vocabulary lists. While they may include other terms, K–12 core vocabulary lists specifically focus on tier two words, which are broad based. When developing these lists, it is important to include words that appear with regularity and that span grade levels, similar to the list of Common Core critical vocabulary.

Words From Literature and Read-Alouds

Read-alouds serve a variety of purposes in a balanced literacy classroom that focuses on reading, writing, and oral language. Reading aloud helps build students' fluency, vocabulary, and comprehension. In addition, read-alouds create the opportunity to introduce students to contextualized words they may not encounter in their independent reading. Read-alouds also provide the important model of an adult reading fluently and with expression; many students do not get to experience such modeling outside school.

We suggest selecting words that are important for understanding the theme of any literary text in addition to targeting tier two words. Targeting words within novels, poems, literature, and picture books provides a great opportunity to introduce words within context and provide incidental word-learning opportunities. In addition to selecting words, teachers can create word lists, anchor charts, or word walls made of words drawn from literature and read-alouds, all of which can provide great opportunities to revisit words.

Spanish Words

Many classrooms and schools welcome an increasing number of Latino students, many of whom are English learners. A simple yet meaningful addition to a print-rich environment is an anchor chart or word wall that features everyday English words along-side their Spanish counterparts. The list of everyday words can include tier one words as well as specific words that are meaningful in the classroom or school, such as *cafeteria*, *gymnasium*, *syllabus*, *assignment*, *notebook*, and so on.

Getting Started on Word Lists

Rather than depending solely on words and word lists determined by textbook pub-lishers, we have attempted to provide a few sound principles to equip teachers and teams to make those selections and embed word learning within their instruction. Teachers can feel confident that, with these intentional choices, they can control which words to teach and how to best teach them.

To begin creating a core vocabulary list, consider creating a shared Google Doc. You may want to create separate documents for K–2 and 3–5 at the elementary level, and classify documents by content areas in middle and high school. Since Google Docs runs in a web browser, you don't need to install any software. The big advantage to sharing a Google Doc as a group is that all files automatically update and save to Google Drive every time a teacher makes a change. Keep in mind that these features work exclusively through Google Drive and don't sync with file-sharing programs like Dropbox, for example. Teams could archive and update word lists by creating a shared notebook in Evernote or OneNote as discussed previously.

Recap

Selecting vocabulary to teach is the first step in a reiterative cycle of actions that takes place within a comprehensive, schoolwide focus on vocabulary development. The ideas and strategies we outline within this chapter will help literacy leadership teams and indi-vidual teachers make more intentional decisions about which words they should teach.

Digital Tools for Selecting Vocabulary Collaboratively

Evernote (https://evernote.com): Digital notebook
OneNote (www.onenote.com): Digital notebook

NEXT STEPS

Consider the following questions individually or discuss them with colleagues or in literacy leadership team settings.

Teachers

- Describe how you currently select vocabulary words. Do you select them yourself, select them with colleagues, or use what the textbook suggests? How does your method align with the strategies presented here?

- How could you apply the tiered framework for selecting and categorizing vocabulary at the grade level or in the discipline you teach?
- Use the reproducible "Sorting Vocabulary Words Into Tiers" on page 36 to practice classifying vocabulary words, and reflect on your responses compared with the responses provided in the answer key.
- Which of the strategies for selecting vocabulary words will you implement?
- Refer to the reproducible "Template for Vocabulary in a Unit of Study" on page 38 for a template to record vocabulary words you've identified and plan instructional strategies.

Literacy Leadership Teams

- Selecting vocabulary is an important consideration and one that teachers often make haphazardly or not at all. How can your leadership team support teachers in purposefully selecting vocabulary?
- Tiered vocabulary is an important concept and one that supports selecting and teaching academic vocabulary. Are your teaching staff members familiar with the tiered framework? If not, how can you help them understand and apply this framework?
- Do you have vertical alignment of targeted vocabulary lists? Do you, as a team, consider this to be important? If so, how could you support that effort? What words would you target for vertical alignment?
- How might your school or district begin applying the five steps outlined in the introduction (page 7) for implementing common schoolwide vocabulary practices?

Sorting Vocabulary Words Into Tiers

Try your hand at sorting vocabulary words into the three tiers we discussed in chapter 3. Read the following terms from a sixth-grade social studies unit about volcanoes, then sort them according to the three tiers. Write the terms in the boxes provided following the terms. Then compare your results with colleagues, and refer to the correct responses on the following page. Keep in mind that there is some subjectivity around placement of specific words into the three tiers, but if a term can be used only in one discipline and only in one specific way, it's definitely a tier three word.

soda bottle	tectonic plates	solid	magma	erupt
expand	geologist	pressure	lava	fall
prediction	smoke	mantle	avalanche	

Tier One: Common Words

Tier Two: Cross-Curricular Words

Tier Three: Technical and Academic Vocabulary

Blended Vocabulary for K–12 Classrooms © 2017 Solution Tree Press • SolutionTree.com
Visit **go.SolutionTree.com/literacy** to download this free reproducible.

Responses for Sorting Vocabulary Words Into Tiers

The terms from the volcano unit are now categorized into the three tiers. Think about how you classified terms and how they compare with the categories below. Discuss with your colleagues or team members.

Tier One: Common Words

smoke

fall

solid

soda bottle

Tier Two: Cross-Curricular Words

pressure

expand

erupt

prediction

Tier Three: Technical and Academic Vocabulary

tectonic plates

magma

lava

geologist

mantle

avalanche

Template for Vocabulary in a Unit of Study

Use this template to determine vocabulary words that will be a focus in the unit of study. In addition, think about appropriate direct and indirect instructional strategies along with digital tools and apps that can support collaboration, practice, and review. You may choose to return to the chapters in this book that are specific to students you teach to define appropriate instructional strategies.

Title of Unit of Study: _____

Vocabulary Words:

Tier Two and Tier Three Focus Words:

Direct Instructional Strategies:

Indirect Strategies:

Digital Tools:

CHAPTER 4

Effective Instruction and Assessment

Planning effective vocabulary instruction takes time and effort. In order to do it intentionally and well, you should consider a few factors and guidelines. In the preceding chapter, we provided criteria to think intentionally about how to classify and select words we want students to know. But after you've selected words, what is the best way to teach them so that students learn them deeply? And after you've taught vocabulary, how do you assess it? Most important is broadening students' vocabulary knowledge and word learning, and we have suggestions to help make that overarching goal seem more doable. The ideas and strategies we outline within this chapter will help literacy leadership teams and individual teachers make more intentional decisions about how to best teach vocabulary words, and how to most ably determine how well students have mastered them. We unpack vocabulary strategies—both direct and indirect—and provide information about the different levels of knowing a word as well as recommendations for how to best instruct students to reach the desired level of mastery and assess their progress in doing so. We then examine ways to assess word learning to ensure these strategies are effective and to inform further instruction as well as the use of additional strategies.

A Balanced Approach to Word Learning

Like so many areas in teaching literacy, achieving balance is key to building a strong and sustainable vocabulary program. A balanced approach to word learning is a viable way to encourage word learning throughout the day in K–12 classrooms. As we see it, there are three specific ways we can blend vocabulary instruction to support students as they expand their word knowledge, deepen their understanding, and begin to use words expressively: (1) provide explicit, effective vocabulary instruction based on years of research, (2) create a literacy environment that supports incidental word learning, and (3) model excellent vocabulary, all the while using digital tools that provide opportunities for practice and review. One of our goals in writing this book is to help teachers teach vocabulary more intentionally. Understanding how to infuse word learning with a blended approach is part of what we mean by being purposeful when selecting strategies and words on which to focus. Let's briefly look at what masquerades as vocabulary instruction but, in fact, *does not* effectively help students build their word knowledge.

What It's Not

Sometimes well-meaning educators think they are teaching vocabulary when, in fact, they are not. Vocabulary programs and long word lists disconnected from classroom practice and authentic context won't create the interest and enthusiasm necessary for building language learners. Before we can think about best practices, we first need to examine a few practices that teachers should retire.

Many teachers simply allow textbook publishers and vocabulary workbooks to become the vocabulary program. Relying solely on words bolded within texts or workbooks to target vocabulary is a well-intentioned, though misguided, effort. Word learning can be so much more than a list of words that students must learn by the end of the week or unit of study. It's not about teaching a list of words that a standardized test maker recommends or focusing only on the targeted words that accompany each chapter, unit, or novel study. And it's definitely not about assigning long lists of words and definitions that students memorize and promptly forget.

A balanced approach doesn't need to include grade-level word lists. While using grade-level lists of words may seem like a good idea, in reality, a well-intentioned teacher can and should select more meaningful words for students. Finally, a focused effort on increasing word learning doesn't have to (and probably shouldn't) include using a vocabulary program, textbook, or workbook with no connection to academic content or curriculum, read-alouds, and independent reading. While this type of vocabulary program serves a limited purpose, overall, we think it abdicates responsibility for the thinking behind word learning and ownership that we can achieve through a more systematic approach.

Effective vocabulary instruction doesn't include having students copy a list of words from a whiteboard, pore over dictionaries, and reproduce tedious definitions. Dictionary definitions are often confusing even when they're connected to more real-world contexts. While dictionaries serve a useful purpose, this type of dreadfully dull, disconnected activity will certainly turn students off of learning words. This activity is about nothing more than copying—not word learning.

Students in many classrooms complete word search puzzles in the guise of reinforcing vocabulary and spelling. Finding words backward, forward, upside down, or diagonally does not reinforce spelling or word meaning. And we know many students who are frustrated doing tasks such as this. While we advocate providing multiple exposures to words in many different ways, word searches don't happen to be one of them.

Teachers can also use word walls ineffectively. Surprised? We'll clarify. We're referring to word walls that teachers prepare before the first day of school, complete with meticulously printed words. The font is large and readable. They may even be color coded by part of speech. Sounds great—right? The only catch is that some word walls appear exactly the same on the final day of school when it's time to dismantle them. While we're huge fans of word walls, intentionality is key. Rather than have them be a static part of the landscape, teachers should develop them purposefully and integrate them with effective instructional activities that support content, independent learning, and review.

Another practice we frequently see is having students mark new words within text or novels with sticky notes. Every single page has several sticky notes, and students sometimes follow a specific protocol that includes looking up the word in a dictionary, copying the definition, and recording a synonym or antonym. While this strategy can be purposeful, it can also quickly become a rote exercise and one that actually becomes disconnected from what real readers do. Again, balance is key. Prescribing any strategy such as this can quickly kill reading enjoyment and word learning.

Worksheets and templates that teachers use to support word learning are another tricky prospect. Some can serve a useful purpose and assist students in thinking more deeply about words. Thinking about what a word reminds you of, what it does not remind you of, and so on can help gradually shift words from receptive to expressive vocabulary. However, similar to sticky notes, too much of a good thing can quickly become a bad thing. And when an acceptable answer is anything that a word reminds one of, then perhaps the purpose behind the strategy has been lost.

The practices described here range from poor to passable in small doses; again, balance and intention are key. Blending direct instructional strategies with a word-filled classroom along with online tools and games creates a rich, multifaceted approach to acquiring a broad vocabulary. Now that we've noted what does *not* contribute to balanced learning, we'll provide suggestions for how to build a cohesive, integrated approach to word learning in your setting. These are general, overarching strategies; you'll find more specific strategies for particular age ranges and populations in chapters 5, 6, and 7.

What It Is

Effective vocabulary instruction includes the following research-based practices (Graves, 2000).

- Teach individual words (additive vocabulary instruction).
- Teach word-learning strategies (generative vocabulary instruction).
- Implement wide reading.
- Foster word consciousness through indirect strategies.

Vocabulary acquisition occurs both directly and indirectly. Schoolwide vocabulary initiatives need to reinforce and encourage both. A balanced vocabulary approach to word learning comprises both direct strategies and indirect strategies to increase word acquisition (National Reading Panel, 2000).

Direct vocabulary learning occurs through explicit instruction of specific words, word study that includes morphology and derivation, and word-learning or meaning-getting strategies. In direct instruction, teachers carefully plan content about words in addition to strategy and skills instruction so students can grow toward becoming more independent word learners and they analyze and decode words, respectively. Direct strategies include intentional word-learning opportunities, and the grade-level or content-specific teacher often plans them. The planner targets these opportunities to support curricular goals, standards, and building general vocabulary.

Indirect strategies are also a critical part of balanced vocabulary instruction. Vocabulary learning thrives within a literacy-rich environment that indirectly supports conversation and oral language activities, reading aloud, shared reading experiences, and wide reading. Think of indirect vocabulary learning as similar to the best literacy learning that begins in the home, when kids learn new words through authentic exposures and through reading and being read to. Indirect strategies in this environment help build word consciousness through conversations, wordplay, and shared and independent reading activities.

While not as targeted as direct instruction, incidental word learning is nevertheless important in a schoolwide vocabulary effort. The variety of strategies included here provides ideas for creating a schoolwide atmosphere that builds word consciousness (Blachowicz & Fisher, 2006; Graves, 2006). The goal is to achieve a balance between planning direct instructional opportunities focused on targeted words and structuring incidental word-learning opportunities throughout the day.

We advocate blending instruction with digital tools that support targeted review of content vocabulary through game-like activities. Rather than thinking of modeling, explicit instruction, indirect or incidental strategies, and digital tools as existing in silos, a blended system integrates the power of each to create a rich, multifaceted approach to vocabulary acquisition. Think of all of these woven together to form a beautiful tapestry.

Elements of Effective Vocabulary Instruction

A comprehensive approach to vocabulary includes an environment that supports rich word learning, targeting words for direct instruction, and teaching students generative strategies to independently learn words. Many digital tools lend themselves well to independent practice and review, and teachers can also integrate many into direct instruction. Technology provides new and alternate ways to differentiate instruction, practice, and review. Now more than ever, students have access to computers and a wide array of mobile devices, which may include tablets, laptops, smartphones, and others. This greater accessibility provides an excellent opportunity for teachers to integrate digital tools into a comprehensive vocabulary program. We're excited about the potential of these web-based tools to increase engagement, differentiation, and practice. We encourage you to take advantage of them and integrate eVoc strategies (Dalton & Grisham, 2011)—those that use technology to promote greater interest in vocabulary—into your classroom instruction and independent practice.

Online reference sources are an important part of independent word learning. In addition to the more traditional reference resources, like dictionaries and glossaries, take time to introduce students to the numerous digital resources available. Web-based tools such as Lingro (www.lingro.com), Lexipedia (www.lexipedia.com), and Snappy Words (www.snappywords.com) are easy for students to use and integrate into their learning routines. Additionally, these online resources provide features such as dynamic visual images and the ability to show relationships among words that are not available in a traditional print resource.

In the following sections, we'll unpack key elements of effective vocabulary instruction and highlight some digital tools that can support them. For each characteristic, see if you can determine whether it's a direct strategy or an indirect means of building student vocabulary.

Create a Literacy-Rich Environment

At their most basic, literacy-rich classroom environments are full of various types of reading materials and environmental print, like signs and anchor charts. A literacy-rich environment, in many ways, is the foundation that supports literacy development, including word learning (Wolfersberger, Reutzel, Sudweeks, & Fawson, 2004). Literacy-rich environments, as endorsed by the International Reading Association and the National Association for the Education of Young Children (1998), have a significant impact on what goes on in the classroom. Additionally, the Common Core State Standards call for increasing the amount of nonfiction and informational text in classrooms (NGA & CCSSO, 2010). A literacy-rich environment not only supports the Common Core and many state and system standards but also provides a setting that encourages and supports speaking, listening, reading, and writing in a variety of authentic ways—through print and digital media (Tyson, 2013e). Depending on student grade level and content area, elements of a literacy-rich environment include, but are not limited to, the following.

- Classroom libraries that include a variety of authors, genres, and text types
- Content posters
- Anchor charts—both teacher made and co-created with students
- Word walls
- Labels
- Literacy workstations
- Writing centers
- Computers, tablets, and handheld digital devices
- Displays of student work
- Displays of books and information
- Bulletin boards

A classroom rich in print and other media can significantly impact literacy learning and help set the stage for increased word learning and improved word consciousness. In addition, research shows a print-rich environment positively affects student achievement (McGill-Franzen, Allington, Yokoi, & Brooks, 1999). *Word consciousness* refers to a variety of cognitive and metacognitive behaviors and a deep understanding of how one uses words effectively both orally and in writing (Blachowicz & Fisher, 2006; Scott, Miller, & Flinspach, 2012). Although incidental word learning is not nearly as targeted as when teachers directly teach specific words, it is nonetheless important. Hart and Risley (1995) document the importance of an environment rich in language to build students' oral vocabulary.

Environmental print refers to the written language that surrounds students in their classrooms. This includes print on classroom walls and other surfaces as well as teacher-made and commercial charts. In our work with schools, we have observed that elementary classrooms are often replete with environmental print. In fact, it sometimes borders on overload, which can distract some students. Purposeful print typically includes labeled areas of the room and objects within the classroom as well as anchor charts, either codeveloped by students and teachers or commercially produced. Elementary classrooms also often include charts with directions, classroom library labels, word walls, and pocket charts filled with individual words, sentences, or poems (Tyson, Cornwell, & Swetnam, 2009). In addition to word walls posted in the classroom, consider using Padlet (https://padlet.com) to create an online, collaborative, digital word wall. Students can participate by adding key words, images, links, and even video clips. It becomes a shared space for collaboration and learning. In classrooms with English learners, develop a shared online word wall that includes images with each word and that students can add to throughout the school year.

The amount and type of environmental print often varies widely from the elementary level to the secondary level. While we somewhat expect this, we think secondary teachers are missing an opportunity to promote and encourage literacy learning. A literacy-rich environment not only is important for developing vocabulary in early learners but supports content-specific learning throughout students' school years. Each element, from word walls to classroom libraries, supports incidental exposure to a variety of words. With the increasing numbers of English learners, labeling the environment makes sense and can benefit students at all levels.

Classrooms rich in print provide the perfect opportunity to flood students with words, which is important in helping students build their general lexicon. Research affirms that students at all levels benefit from literacy-rich, word-conscious classrooms where teachers are eager to discuss new words and fill their rooms with books, word games, dictionaries, and digital and print media that provide an environment for vocabulary growth (Blachowicz & Fisher, 2004).

Provide Multiple Exposures to New Vocabulary

Providing multiple exposures to new words is one of the single most important things to remember to do when creating word-learning routines. Word learning is not a one-and-done activity. That's why depending on long lists of words—often quickly memorized before a quiz—doesn't work for long-term vocabulary development. Research has long documented the importance of multiple exposures to words over time (McKeown, Beck, Omanson, & Pople, 1985; Stahl, 2005; Stahl & Fairbanks, 1986). Students can learn new words through varied opportunities, including reading, writing, speaking, and listening.

Remembering that students have both an expressive and receptive vocabulary is crucial to understanding why numerous exposures are necessary. Words will only move from a student's receptive vocabulary (understood when listening and reading) to expressive vocabulary (used in speaking and writing) after many opportunities to hear, practice, review, and use words within a variety of formal and informal settings. When students become more familiar with how words are used in various contexts, they'll be more likely to try using them. Since the goal is to have students use new words when speaking and writing, revisiting targeted words and providing a wide range of opportunities—both linguistic and nonlinguistic—to develop a nuanced understanding of words are important.

With intentionality, teachers can control which words to teach in a cursory manner, which specific terms to teach in depth, and how to best teach all words. Above all, it is essential to keep in mind that teachers shape word meaning through multiple exposures. In other words, regardless of the specific words they select for any particular purpose, they should foster plenty of opportunities for students to engage with new vocabulary over time.

Target Specific Words

A comprehensive vocabulary program always includes direct instruction on targeted words. While it is impossible to teach all the words students need to know, researchers estimate that teachers can explicitly teach about four hundred words per year in school (Beck et al., 2013). Teachers determine which words students need most and engage them in meaningful activities around these preselected words. Teachers should feel confident in targeting specific words for direct instruction. When selecting words, teachers frequently ask the valid question, "Which words should I choose?" Our simple response is that it depends on your learning goals.

For example, academic texts include much more specialized vocabulary that will hinder comprehension if students don't understand it. We know from research that vocabulary knowledge makes a big difference when comprehending connected text (Stahl & Fairbanks, 1986). To make sure students can understand these texts, selecting highly technical words (tier three) makes sense. On the other hand, teachers may choose to focus on teaching tier two words (Beck et al., 2013), which broaden students' understanding across content areas and in a variety of contexts.

Frontload Vocabulary

Teaching targeted vocabulary can take a variety of forms. Frontloading, or preteaching, can be particularly important before students engage with challenging, academic text. Frontloading vocabulary can be as simple as drawing students' attention to several key words before reading a selection, listening to a lecture, or viewing a video.

Teachers can frontload vocabulary in several ways. One simple routine includes pronouncing the word; providing a simple, student-friendly definition; and displaying the correct spelling so that students can see what it actually looks like. Teachers can elicit students' background knowledge and lead a short discussion about how to use the word within context. With this routine, in a brief amount of time, students build background knowledge and become familiar with words that they may otherwise pass over or ignore because of unfamiliarity. And, when students recognize and understand vocabulary from the text they are reading, their comprehension increases (Pressley, Disney, & Anderson, 2007).

Providing visual images is another easy way to frontload vocabulary. Teachers can target words with visual dictionaries such as Shahi (http://blachan.com/shahi), Snappy Words (www.snappywords.com), and Visual Dictionary Online (http://visual.merriam-webster .com). Visual images help most students, and can be essential for English learners. More information about each visual dictionary is available in appendix A (page 107).

Teach Independent Word-Learning Strategies

In addition to learning words through direct instruction, students must also engage in word-learning strategies that enable them to independently determine word meaning in varied contexts. In a comprehensive approach to vocabulary, most vocabulary researchers point to three strategies to help students independently determine the meaning of unfamiliar words: (1) use of context, (2) use of word parts, and (3) use of reference materials (Graves, 2006, 2007). We find the first two strategies noted here to be the most effective and will limit our discussion to focus on them. When encountering unfamiliar words, students can use context clues and morphemic analysis (focusing on prefixes, suffixes, and root words) to determine meaning if they don't reach for a reference source.

While many other areas of research are clear, it is worth noting that the research on the effectiveness of word-learning strategies is limited and reveals mixed results. Some studies show benefits, and others do not. It is clear that good readers seem to understand word parts and use these to determine word meanings as they read. Again, the more students read, the better readers they become. So, how do we help students who tend to read less develop a useful understanding of word parts? Many teachers routinely direct students to use context to determine word meaning. However, using context can be tricky and sometimes unreliable. Context is more helpful and straightforward when reading informational text than in novels, in which context may be less clear. The study of word parts (affixes, prefixes, and Greek and Latin root words) develops most significantly between fourth grade and high school, and we believe these word parts should receive attention in a comprehensive vocabulary effort (Nagy, Diakidoy, & Anderson, 1993). James F. Baumann and his colleagues (2002) repeatedly find that students who learn morphemic analysis skills become more proficient at learning new words independently.

In order for students to develop independence in using word parts and context, they need direct, scaffolded instruction with lots of guided practice. In thinking about how to approach an instructional routine, Mark B. Pacheco and Amanda P. Goodwin (2013) suggest the following strategies.

- Encourage chunking words into meaningful parts, beginning with the largest known word or chunk (for example, *hyper* + *sensitive* + *ity*).
- Provide opportunities for students to make connections between words and word units, such as *trans*, *hyper*, or *ology*.
- Practice morphology within the context of what students are reading.
- Help students make connections to languages they may be learning.

As part of a districtwide emphasis on vocabulary, providing repeated practice in using context and root words, prefixes, and suffixes seems promising to equip students in grades 4 through 12 to more readily tackle the complex vocabulary of academic texts.

Actively Engage Students

Teachers need to actively engage students in learning new words and encourage them to control their own word learning. Engagement is important in that it highly correlates with vocabulary learning as well as other areas of literacy learning (Campbell, Voelkl, & Donahue, 2000). Shifting words from receptive to expressive vocabulary requires practicing, reviewing, listening to, reading, and often playing with words.

Teachers can stimulate students to revisit words to review and expand meaning in many different ways. For example, filling the classroom with commercial word games such as Boggle and Scrabble and reviewing words in a game-like fashion helps students extend their understanding of words and how to use them. In addition, many digital tools can engage students and provide great opportunities that support and extend word learning, practice, and review.

Including digital tools can also provide a means for students to actively engage in practice, review, and expansion of their vocabulary. For example, Flashcard Stash (http://flashcardstash.com) is a tool teachers and students can use to quickly review words and save missed words to review again. Teachers can use the website Vocabulary Games (www.vocabulary.co.il) on a whiteboard and help students at all levels review synonyms and antonyms or build their vocabulary for the ACT and SAT examinations. Other tools such as Free Rice (www.freerice.com) are fun and game-like, as students match words to the correct definition, which causes a virtual bowl to fill with rice. The site then donates actual rice to those in need. For additional tools, see appendix A (page 107), which we devote to an in-depth analysis and review of more than twenty-five digital tools that provide interactive ways to reinforce word learning and that teachers can easily incorporate into a vocabulary routine.

Advocate for Wide Reading

Students have many words to learn. Researchers estimate that they learn an average of three to four thousand words per year (D'Anna, Zechmeister, & Hall, 1991; Nagy & Herman, 1987). And we can agree that it is impossible to directly teach students more than a small fraction of that number. It stands to reason that much of this growth occurs through reading, listening, discussion, and interacting with people and media. Wide reading has been the subject of much research, and studies suggest that incidental word learning occurs through independent reading (Nagy, Anderson, & Herman, 1987; Nagy et al., 1985).

Because independent reading plays a direct role in growing vocabulary, we need to ensure students engage in independent reading across classrooms. Two of the prerequisites necessary for independent reading include time and text. In other words, the schedule must allow for it, and there must be digital or print books available to read, ideally from a classroom library.

When teachers provide well-designed classroom libraries including print and digital resources, students interact more with books, spend more time reading, demonstrate more positive attitudes toward reading, and exhibit higher levels of reading achievement (Grigg, Daane, Jin, & Campbell, 2003). Independent reading time with self-chosen materials is important not only for students who perform well but also for those who struggle with reading. Relegating students to selecting books from rigid Lexile levels neither promotes interest and engagement nor challenges and expands students' vocabulary. We suggest creating classroom structures and routines that support independent reading as a viable means to build vocabulary.

Engage in Read-Alouds

Read-alouds, another incidental means of building vocabulary, often take a backseat to more direct instructional approaches. Educators accept that reading books with students, especially early learners, builds vocabulary. Many classrooms are filled with leveled texts. With early learners, reading high-quality picture books provides the advantage of exposing students to a much more advanced, complex level of vocabulary than students see within leveled texts (Bond & Wasik, 2009; Connor, Morrison, & Slominski, 2006). For example, students may not encounter words such as *prow*, *figureheads*, *conservatory*, *tropical*, *satisfaction*, *headlands*, and *lupines* in everyday conversation with friends and family, but they would hear them when listening to a teacher or parent read *Miss Rumphius* (Cooney, 1982). Similarly, intermediate students would not readily hear words such as *blithely*, *umbrage*, *discern*, *domestic*, or *derogatory* used orally among their peers or family; however, they would hear them as their teacher read aloud *The Miraculous Journey of Edward Tulane* (DiCamillo, 2006). In addition to higher-level words, picture books include illustrations that often represent interesting words in the text that help students understand new vocabulary in context (Ganea, Pickard, & DeLoache, 2008). However, simply reading books aloud to students isn't enough to advance word learning. When reading, teachers need to specifically draw attention to words within context and provide simple, student-friendly definitions and conversation around higher-level vocabulary. We define and explore strategies for early learners in chapter 5.

Create Rich Language Experiences

Although incidental word learning is not nearly as targeted as when teachers directly teach specific words, it is nonetheless important. Hart and Risley (1995) document the importance of an environment rich in language to build students' oral vocabulary. The classroom teacher must orchestrate many rich language experiences, because no one on staff can be sure of what language students experience beyond the classroom, school, and playground. The words we use in our everyday conversation and instruction with our students are critical. For example, when giving instructions repeatedly, we can use synonyms so that students hear unfamiliar words alongside familiar ones. Something as simple as calling a pencil a *pencil* in one sentence and a *writing implement* in the next sentence models naming objects in different ways. Media specialists, food service staff, and other personnel can help build rich language experiences for students as well. We have worked in numerous schools that display word walls in the library, gymnasiums, and hallways, and include terms like *arugula* or *al dente* on lunchroom menus. Simple acts like these heighten awareness of specific words and discreetly urge students to engage in conversation about them.

Vocabulary Assessment

To gauge whether these strategies have been effective, determine whether they need adjustments, decide whether to implement new strategies, and even to understand students' prior knowledge, teachers must assess students' word learning. In the following sections, we share information about ascertaining student learning throughout the stages of vocabulary acquisition, and several different formats and tools that are conducive to assessing vocabulary.

Four Stages of Word Learning

As teachers, it isn't enough to simply understand that helping students build diverse vocabulary knowledge is important. When teaching vocabulary, it's important to determine your students' level of familiarity and understanding of the targeted words (the words students must learn and that teachers teach during a lesson segment); it's useful information for students to understand as well.

How do you easily determine how well students understand words? Knowing a word's meaning isn't as simple as "I know it" or "I don't." What does it really mean to know a word? More often than not, a student's word knowledge lies somewhere along a continuum of understanding. Edgar Dale (1965) developed one of the earliest and most respected descriptions of this continuum. He describes the four stages of word development, which we'll unpack into practical terms.

1. The student has no knowledge of the word; he or she has never heard or seen the word.
2. The student may have heard the word, but he or she doesn't really know what it means.

3. The student can make general associations with the word and recognize it within context.

4. The student has a rich understanding of the word and can use it when he or she speaks and writes.

As a teacher, you can fairly easily determine how well students understand words by keeping in mind these four distinct stages (Dale, 1965). The progression is similar to turning on a dimmer switch. With each stage, the light—that is, the student's understanding—becomes brighter.

In order to illustrate the four stages, consider a teacher who is teaching her students the meaning of the term *polygon* in mathematics. Some students will have never heard or seen the word *polygon*. (This is stage 1; the dimmer switch is off.) Another group of students may remember hearing the word but can't tell the meaning. In other words, they may remember hearing a teacher use the word *polygon* but don't remember what it means. (This is stage 2; the light is very dim.) Still another group of students can make general associations with the term and place it within a category, which denotes a higher level of understanding. They may, for example, remember that a polygon is a shape they learned about in mathematics class. (This is stage 3; the light is getting brighter.) And, finally, some students can use the word. In other words, they can express that a polygon is a flat shape with at least three closed lines. (This is stage 4; the light is bright.) In keeping with the example of the dimmer switch, as a student becomes more secure in his or her understanding of the term *polygon*, the switch gradually moves as the student deepens his or her understanding from stage 1 to stage 4, showing that he or she can use the word appropriately.

Not only do you need to know and understand what each stage looks like, but it is recommended that you teach your students this information as well. To become independent learners, students benefit from gauging their own knowledge of specific words as they build their vocabularies.

Let's move a step further and explore how to use the four stages of word learning as a formative assessment tool. We must orient primary students to each stage by providing numerous examples. We recommend creating an anchor chart with students and posting it in the classroom to serve as a reference. See figure 4.1 for an example of an anchor chart. Using several examples, students can provide feedback specific to their stage of word learning by raising one to four fingers, indicating their level of understanding for any given word.

For intermediate and secondary students, we suggest using a simple chart or creating a template that students can access on a laptop or mobile device. Before a unit of study, for example, display your preselected vocabulary words online or on a whiteboard. As a teacher pronounces each word and provides a brief definition or synonym, he or she can have students record the word in the category that best describes their knowledge of each word. He or she then circulates around the room and sees in which categories students have written words on their template. The teacher will quickly gain a good idea

Title or Content: _____

Directions: Read the words at the bottom of the page or on the whiteboard. After you read each one, write the word in the column that best describes how much you know about each one.

Phase 1	Phase 2	Phase 3	Phase 4
I don't know the word at all.	I have seen or heard the word; I don't know the meaning.	I think I know the meaning (I might know the meaning in context).	I know the meaning.

Figure 4.1: How Well Do I Know These Words? anchor chart.

of students' familiarity with the terms. For students, this activity can serve as a quick check to help them get a clear picture of how much practice they may need to master the unit vocabulary. Students can use the chart later while reviewing to determine whether they learned the words well enough to move to phases 3 and 4. The goal, of course, is for students to become independent word learners, fully aware of when they know or don't know a word's meaning and how to transform unknown words to words they can use expressively. There are several additional forms of assessment that teachers can use to evaluate students' vocabulary knowledge in order to move them closer to mastery.

Assessment Formats

Nicole Dimich Vagle (2015) defines assessment as an "intentional process of gathering information, both formal and informal, to understand a student's learning and performance in order to facilitate and communicate achievement and levels of proficiency" (p. 10). Assessing word learning is, in short, a tricky issue. Many teachers grapple with it as they implement effective vocabulary instruction. However, it's important. An important consideration to guide you through this process is to remember to always consider your purpose. Ask yourself, in other words, "What do I want to learn from the assessment?" For example, you may want to see if students can use words when speaking or writing. In a classroom rich in print, language, and conversation, informal assessment may be more useful and easier to manage, and may provide more actionable information than formal assessment. There are also occasions when you need to know a student's general vocabulary knowledge, or times when you may want to determine if students can recognize words within context. Simpler yet, you may need to determine how well students have learned words that you explicitly targeted and taught.

While each of these objectives is valid, it's necessary to determine your purpose before selecting or developing an assessment. In the sections that follow, we'll highlight assessment formats that can help you learn more about your students' word use and knowledge in order to help them better achieve deep understanding and application.

Standardized Assessments

At times, educators seek to measure general vocabulary knowledge. The fourth edition of the Peabody Picture Vocabulary Test (PPVT-4; Dunn & Dunn, 2007), a long-standing and widely used standardized measure, helps educators assess a student's receptive vocabulary knowledge. The PPVT-4 is made up of multiple-choice items that show four pictures for each vocabulary word; the student selects the picture that best illustrates the definition of the word. The PPVT-4 is particularly well suited to assess students' vocabulary acquisition (Rice & Watkins, 1996) but has been nationally standardized using various age groups ranging from two years old to ninety and above.

The Nelson-Denny Reading Test is a reading survey test for high school students, college students, and adults. Kimberly used this measure frequently when working in developmental education programs at the college and university level. The Nelson-Denny provides a measure in three areas: (1) vocabulary, (2) comprehension, and (3) reading rate. It is often used for placement purposes and, using alternate forms, as a pre- and post-test measure of growth in these areas. Students or others can complete the Nelson-Denny, typically administered on a computer, in forty-five minutes.

While both of these instruments can provide general information about an individual's vocabulary knowledge, it is important to remember that they are not assessments of vocabulary learning. Rather, they measure general vocabulary knowledge accumulated over time, which can provide general information useful for limited purposes. They may provide interesting data as a baseline measure or for placement decisions, but you should never consider either of them as a complete picture of a student's vocabulary knowledge.

Cloze Assessments

The word *cloze* is derived from *clozentropy*, which is the technique of removing words from a text so that a reader attempts to fill in the blanks with known words and concepts. Cloze tasks require students to determine the word or words that best fit within the sentence according to the context. Cloze assessments can be either closed or open. *Closed cloze* items, in which a target word appears along with several *distractors* (incorrect answers) from which students choose, are suitable for use in a content-area class where a teacher has taught specific terms. As a vocabulary task, students use background experience with the word along with semantic clues, syntactic understanding, and receptive word knowledge to determine the correct word choice. *Open cloze* items require the learner to supply a word without being given choices. They require a much higher level of word knowledge and understanding of semantic and syntactic clues.

Student Writing

Many well-meaning teachers have assigned students a targeted list of words to learn—sometimes spelling words—as part of a weekly routine. At some point during the week, students are typically expected to use the targeted words within sentences. And the sentences that students write end up looking something like the following example (italicized words reflect the target word).

- He *frolicked*.
- My mother *frolicked*.
- My dog *frolicked*.
- They *frolicked* in the park. (Lest the teacher catch on to the pattern.)

We have observed teachers of all grade levels assigning similar tasks, and Kimberly's two children have brought home these sorts of assignments year after year.

While teachers intend for students to practice using vocabulary within a written context, thinking about how people acquire vocabulary quickly reveals why this task doesn't fit the learning goal. You'll recall that word learning is a gradual process and one that occurs with exposures over time. The final stage in learning new words is to be able to use those words in speaking and writing (expressive vocabulary). Put simply, students often have too little experience to be able to use a list of words and write meaningful sentences immediately. This lack of experience is precisely why students often write sentences using repetitive patterns such as those shown in the example list we provided that end up making little or no sense (but sometimes make us laugh).

Student writing is, in fact, a good measure of word knowledge and use. Rather than assign students to write contrived sentences, consider activities that provide them with more ownership over their writing, such as keeping vocabulary notebooks (print or digital) in which they add new words, engaging in quick writes using targeted vocabulary, or writing within ongoing response journals. All of these activities not only help students think more carefully about how to use the words they select but also keep word learning recursive.

Formative Assessments

As educators teach selected words and provide multiple exposures to them, it's important to check for understanding (Fisher & Frey, 2007) and incorporate quick assessments to determine where students fall on the continuum of knowing a word. Additionally, teachers can quickly clear up misconceptions about identifying and using specific vocabulary words accurately in oral and written language.

There are numerous simple ways to determine how well students understand key vocabulary related to a unit of study. For example, teachers can use paper exit tickets on which students record definitions of key vocabulary. They can also have students practice using new vocabulary in discussion with one another and listen in on conversations in order to quickly assess vocabulary use.

Teachers can also use digital tools for formative assessment purposes. The advantage of digital tools is not only the engagement factor but the ease with which they allow teachers to quickly check for understanding. There are several online tools that can provide feedback for teachers and students. Visit **go.SolutionTree.com/literacy** for live links to these resources.

- **Twitter:** A Twitter (https://twitter.com) feed can serve as an exit ticket. Using a class hashtag, students can tweet the meaning of key academic vocabulary.

Teachers can quickly scan the feed to see if students are on the right track with their understanding.

- **Kahoot!:** Kahoot! (https://getkahoot.com) is a free, game-like classroom-response tool that engages participants and provides feedback in real time. Teachers can use Kahoot! to build multiple-choice quizzes for students to access from their computers, laptops, or other mobile devices. To use it as an assessment tool, teachers could write a sentence and have students select the correct word from four target words that would be correctly used within the context of the sentence. Kimberly frequently uses Kahoot! in professional learning sessions, and participants love it. To learn more about creating a free account and using it in your classroom, watch the YouTube video *How to Use Kahoot! in the Classroom* (Tech in 2, 2014).

- **Socrative:** Another tool that teachers can use for formative assessment purposes with intermediate and secondary students is Socrative (www.socrative.com). Teachers can use this digital tool to develop quick quizzes, exit tickets, and game-like activities to gain a better understanding of students' understanding of specific words. Space Race, a game-like tool on the Socrative website, is fun for students as they compete in teams. The website divides students into teams, and they can track their progress and correct responses by watching rockets race one another. This provides teachers with valuable information about students' understanding of important vocabulary.

- **Plickers:** So, what if each student doesn't have a mobile device or laptop? Plickers (www.plickers.com) is a digital tool that doesn't require each student to be logged on using a mobile device. Instead, the teacher creates a card for each student that contains a large square resembling a simplified QR code. The four sides of the square that make up the code are labeled A, B, C, and D. After the teacher asks a question, students hold up their cards so that the letter they choose to answer the question with is at the top of their card. Using the camera on a smartphone, the teacher quickly takes a picture of the class. The app will code in the students' names and answers, and the teacher sees the name of each student and whether he or she got the answer (or vocabulary word, in this case) correct.

Class Discussions

Classroom discussions provide yet another informal way to determine how well students understand and are able to use key vocabulary words when speaking informally with classmates. Within academic classes, teachers frequently pose questions and use discussion starters as an impetus for small-group discussion on key topics. Employing a protocol or rubric for observation, teachers can record words and concepts students use within their interactions. This quick, informal measure can provide solid information based on students' discussions with classmates to help teachers adjust instruction.

Recap

Vocabulary instruction is more important in the lives of 21st century students than ever before. Our increasingly complex society requires a high level of aptitude in literacy activities, including reading, writing, speaking, and listening. Weaving the elements of effective vocabulary instruction and assessment into classroom routines will help ensure that students are exposed to a rich, wide range of words. Appropriate assessment of vocabulary learning that involves students will help guide teachers and learners in their vocabulary acquisition journey. Creating an environment across classrooms that supports incidental and intentional word learning is critical in educating our students for lifelong success.

Digital Tools for Effective Instruction and Assessment

Flashcard Stash (http://flashcardstash.com): Games and review
Free Rice (www.freerice.com): Games and review
Kahoot! (https://getkahoot.com): Formative assessment and review tool
Lexipedia (www.lexipedia.com): Visual thesaurus
Lingro (www.lingro.com): Dictionary
Padlet (https://padlet.com): Digital word wall
Plickers (www.plickers.com): Formative assessment and review tool
Shahi (http://blachan.com/shahi): Visual dictionary
Snappy Words (www.snappywords.com): Visual thesaurus
Socrative (www.socrative.com): Formative assessment and review tool
Twitter (https://twitter.com): Social media
Visual Dictionary Online (http://visual.merriam-webster.com): Online dictionary including images to accompany words
Vocabulary Games (www.vocabulary.co.il): Practice and review tool

NEXT STEPS

Consider the following questions individually or discuss them with colleagues or in literacy leadership team settings.

Teachers

- Think about the concept of a balanced approach to word learning. How would you describe your classroom? Is there balance? Why or why not?
- Reflect on what effective vocabulary instruction *is* and *isn't*. Did anything surprise you? Are there any practices that you will consider abandoning in favor of more effective practices?
- Which direct instructional strategies do you currently use? How can you include more?
- Select a direct instructional strategy that you will try with your students.
- What types of indirect activities do you engage in with your students? Which have you found most beneficial?
- Select an indirect instructional strategy that you can incorporate in your classroom. How will you go about implementing this strategy?

- The characteristics of effective vocabulary instruction can go a long way toward integrating meaningful word learning in your classroom. Which of the characteristics do you currently employ? Are there some that you can strengthen?
- With colleagues, discuss the assessment strategies presented and how each aligns with word learning.
- Name an assessment strategy that would support the instructional cycle in your classroom or content area. Why did you select this strategy?
- Is there a digital assessment tool that you could easily incorporate to check for understanding?
- How could you use the tool in figure 4.1 (page 51) practically within your classroom?

Literacy Leadership Teams

- Discuss what effective vocabulary instruction is and isn't with colleagues. Have you observed any of the nonproductive practices in your school? What can the team do to nudge these practices in the right direction?
- Teaching vocabulary effectively both explicitly and indirectly is important in schoolwide implementation. Briefly describe the differences between direct and indirect strategies.
- Which strategies do you notice teachers using more frequently in your school—direct or indirect strategies?
- If you were going to select several strategies—both explicit and indirect—to weave into your schoolwide approach to vocabulary, which would they be? Why?
- Consider focusing on the elements of effective vocabulary instruction for several faculty meetings. We encourage the team to develop a wiki, Pinterest board, LiveBinder, or other online collection area to share ideas and strategies specific to each characteristic. Or, you could develop questions and conversation around these characteristics as part of a Twitter chat.
- Talk about how to integrate web-based tools to build vocabulary with more traditional teaching methods. How can you help teachers as they try to integrate online tools?
- How do you plan to support teachers and monitor implementation?
- Consider introducing several digital tools for formative assessment purposes. Which one would you start with? Try integrating Kahoot!, for example, within a professional learning session with teachers.

CHAPTER 5

Vocabulary Strategies for Elementary Students

Elementary teachers face a gargantuan task. Their roles are varied and diverse. When students enter kindergarten, there is often a wide gap in their levels of familiarity with oral and written language. Louisa Cook Moats (2001), a well-respected researcher, referred to this gap in word knowledge and confusion around word meanings as *word poverty*. As we discussed previously, word poverty directly impacts early literacy learning. One of the primary responsibilities of teachers who instruct elementary students is to help them become proficient and fluent readers who read widely with both pleasure and comprehension. Before teachers can achieve that, they must also ensure that students have the largest possible oral vocabulary.

Teachers may wonder if vocabulary instruction differs greatly with students of different ages. In short, it does not differ very much, except that the majority of elementary students' output or application of vocabulary is verbal, especially at ages four and five. Effective vocabulary instruction should always be engaging and include meaningful, student-friendly definitions; context for words; images when appropriate; and ample time for talking about words. With primary-grades students, writing plays less of a role than with intermediate students, while context is likely to be more important. In this chapter, we summarize strategies that are well suited for building vocabulary in elementary learners—speaking, listening, reading, and writing skills. In addition, we highlight digital tools that support word learning for elementary students, since technology and mobile devices are increasingly a part of their everyday lives. Widespread technology (classrooms equipped with tablets, for example) provides additional literacy learning opportunities integrated with print activities without the time constraint of more traditional computer labs (Brand & Kinash, 2010). As always, the wisdom of teachers is paramount here. If you can envision an adjustment to one of these strategies that might make it more useful for your younger (or older) students, then you should certainly experiment and see how things play out in your classroom.

Motor Imaging

Young learners love to move—both when we want them to and when we don't. Motor imaging (Casale, 1985) is one of our favorite nonlinguistic strategies that reinforces word learning through physical movements. At its core, students link the linguistic meaning of the target word with a psychomotor action, creating a multimodal association engaging both body and mind. The following five steps outline this process.

1. The teacher introduces the target word and provides the definition (linguistic).
2. Each student chooses and demonstrates his or her own simple pantomime or gesture (nonlinguistic).
3. The teacher selects a common gesture and demonstrates for all to see.
4. Students repeat the word while doing the common class expression.
5. The class engages with text that uses the target word in context.

The following example demonstrates how Kimberly uses these motor-imaging steps with a group of third-grade students who are about to read a story that uses the word *abode* frequently. She anticipates that most students will not be familiar with this synonym for *home*.

1. Kimberly says, "Boys and girls, in the story we're reading today, you'll hear the characters referring to an *abode*." After asking students if anyone could provide a meaning for the word, she goes on to provide the meaning of *abode* as another word for *home*.
2. Kimberly says, "Using your body, show me how you would remember the word *abode*." Some students use their arms and form a simple house shape, while many others use their hands to form the outline of a house.
3. After scanning the room, Kimberly says, "Most of you used your hands to make the shape of a triangle that looks something like this. It sort of looks like the roof of a house." Kimberly demonstrates the common gesture or movement for *abode*.
4. Next, Kimberly says, "Do it with me. Each time we read the word *abode* in the story, use your hands to show me *abode*." Students show *abode* with their hands.
5. Kimberly goes on to read the story while students use their hands to represent *abode* each time the word appears in the story.

At its core, motor imaging is a great example of a nonlinguistic strategy. In practice, it is easy to integrate, students quickly take to it, and it provides an energetic way to reinforce word learning.

A cautionary note, however: do not choose more than a few words that are integral to the text's meaning when using this strategy before reading. In the example we shared, Kimberly chose the word *abode* because it is central to understanding the story. She could have included a couple of other target words, but in this example, one word and its corresponding gesture from students was plenty for them to concentrate on as they engaged in shared reading. We've seen teachers with good intentions preteach five or so words in this fashion, but students get so preoccupied with which gesture to do when that their comprehension suffers. This strategy is meant to enhance comprehension, not simply to allow for movement and fun.

Concept Circle

The concept circle, first introduced by Richard T. Vacca and Jo Anne L. Vacca (1986) and popularized by Janet Allen (2007), is another strategy that works well for learning and associating words in the increased amount of informational text students now interact with. The big idea behind the concept circle is that, while informational text is organized around concepts or topics, central ideas, and details including facts, understanding rests on vocabulary knowledge. This simple graphic organizer helps students analyze connections between words and explain relationships among these words and the topic. We've found it works well with elementary and secondary students depending on the topic and the words selected (Tyson, 2012b).

As a visual organizer, the concept circle helps students categorize words related to a concept or topic. It is simply a circle divided into four sections. Students record a word in each section as it relates to the concept. See figure 5.1 for an example. In addition to categorizing words, students should explain connections between those words either in writing or orally.

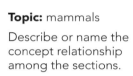
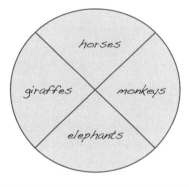

Topic: mammals

Describe or name the concept relationship among the sections.

Figure 5.1: Concept circle on mammals.

Teachers with the best of intentions can still sometimes get so caught up in teaching vocabulary that students may learn many new words without seeing the connections between them and the overarching concept or topic. When using concept circles, teachers can compel students to think carefully about those connections.

You can use concept circles in a variety of ways—for discussion, quick checks, assessment, and more. At the primary level, students can easily use them with more teacher direction. At the intermediate or secondary level, you can use them to check for understanding, promote discussion about terms, and have students quiz one another. Students can also use them in their vocabulary journals to process academic terms as they learn them.

For younger students—or students who struggle with vocabulary and comprehension at any level—you may wish to try this slightly simpler version of the concept circle, which we call a *word wheel*. The wheel is divided into three sections—a half circle on the left-hand side and two quarters of a circle on the right-hand side. You can quickly sketch this visual or give it to students on paper. Write the target word in the left-hand "slice" of the wheel, and use the two slices on the right-hand side for synonyms or pictures. When Angela uses this strategy with students in grade 3 and higher, she usually provides one synonym for the top right slice and then asks students to co-create a synonym for the lower right slice. With younger students, teachers usually place a quickly drawn sketch in the top right slice and a very simple synonym in the bottom right. See figure 5.2 for an example from a fifth-grade class that encounters the word *cricket* while reading the book *Wilfrid Gordon McDonald Partridge* by Australian author Mem Fox (1989).

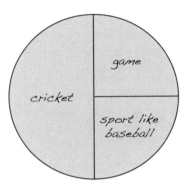

Figure 5.2: Word wheel example.

*Visit **go.SolutionTree.com/literacy** for a free reproducible version of this figure.*

Word Walls

An essential part of a print-rich environment, word walls offer a rich vocabulary resource for students and serve as a teaching and learning tool. Word walls function as more than a place to display words. You can use them to effectively support and extend word learning for students from kindergarten through twelfth grade. Create word walls with students, change them up frequently, and use them as a resource for students to build a strong and diverse vocabulary.

While word walls may include high-frequency words arranged in alphabetical order, they can and should serve more purposes than that. There are endless ways to organize and display them. Word walls come in varied forms—portable and digital, in the hallway and on a traditional classroom wall. They will differ depending on several factors, including the grade level, content area, student population, and perhaps location.

Kimberly outlines five simple steps to use when working with teachers to help make word walls better support word learning (Tyson, 2013a): (1) create word walls with your students, (2) display them your way, (3) change up your word walls, (4) add images to accompany words, and (5) review and play games.

Step 1: Create Word Walls With Your Students

It is common for elementary teachers to work diligently to make their classrooms picture perfect in preparation for back-to-school night. In doing so, they often create the ultimate word wall complete with neatly printed words. However, we suggest that you resist the urge to use fancy fonts or laminate them—this serves no purpose for the students and only takes more of your precious time. Also, there is no need to place labels on bookshelves, tables, centers, and so forth. Rather, inform parents that you'll be working with students to pepper the room with print as the year progresses.

Instead of making word walls independently, create them (yes, more than one!) with your students. Perhaps you need a word wall for mathematics terms, and another one for literary terms. Or perhaps you'll develop one for read-alouds and another in the shape of a large, flowering plant, because that's what the current science unit focuses on. It's really up to you, and there's no limit to your imagination. Whatever will best support the learning of critical (and current) content is what will best serve you and your students.

As the year progresses, select your words from content units, high-frequency words, must-know words, and more! Focus most of your word walls on tier two and tier three vocabulary words; however, if you have a high number of English learners in your school, you'll want word walls that include everyday words (tier one) as well. Remember to frequently change the words displayed to stay current with your content. Also, routinely retire words once the majority of your students know them to make room for ones they are still learning. Retiring words can be a fun joint activity to do with students. Students can provide input as to whether they really know the word.

As you develop your word walls, write the words in large, simple letters with a wide-tip black marker, or print in an easy-to-read font like Arial or Calibri. Resist the urge to laminate words. You want students to *use* and *refer to* the word walls from across the room; too often, the glare of laminated vocabulary cards in fluorescent lights makes them unreadable. Also, words need only be displayed in alphabetical order for primary students; older students who have mastered the alphabet don't need this support. For older students, simply group words in a way that makes sense for the content. Grouping words conceptually makes much more sense and provides rich language opportunities for students.

Step 2: Display Them Your Way

Classroom space is limited in many schools. If you're short on wall space to display word walls, get creative. Just as there is no one right way to *create* a word wall, there is no one right way to *display* a word wall either. Here are a few ideas.

- **Portable word walls:** Think about having separate areas or creating portable word walls for categories or groups of words. You can write words on standing charts, on the outside of large boxes that you or students can turn to show various sides, and numerous other places.
- **Cupboard doors:** No wall space? Use cupboard or closet doors to display words. They're not as wide but work quite well. You can also use windows, avoiding any parts that may open (and thus prevent visibility when opened).

- **Ceiling tiles:** We've seen a few teachers use paper clips and hang words from ceiling tiles or create word mobiles with coat hangers and strings loaded with related words. Not only is it creative, but it works!
- **Pocket chart:** Use a pocket chart to create a simple and easily changeable word wall. Displaying words in pocket charts has the advantage of allowing students to easily group and regroup words according to concepts, stages of knowing a word, and so on.
- **Tall cabinet or file cabinet:** Both of these can be a great, usable space to display words of all types. Just stick a small magnet on the back of each word and, voila, you have a word wall.
- **Anchor charts:** Create portable word walls on chart paper. You can easily create them for each unit or content theme. Then hang them on rings on a chart stand so students can flip through and refer to them as needed when stored in a specified area of the classroom.
- **Other methods:** A quick search for *word walls* or *word walls in the classroom* on Pinterest (www.pinterest.com) yields additional ideas for your consideration.

Step 3: Change Up Your Word Walls

It's easy to create a word wall in September and, over time, forget about it until it's time to dismantle the classroom in May. Word walls can easily become part of the scenery, so to speak, instead of a useful, intentional tool to support literacy learning. So, change them up!

Here are a few ideas for alternative content for your word walls.

- Phonic patterns
- Nonlinguistic hallway word walls
- Spelling, word family, and rhyming patterns
- Content, topical, or thematic word walls
- Words students know
- Prefixes, suffixes, and root words
- Words from read-alouds
- Spanish or English word walls
- Graffiti word walls (words that students find during reading or listening that are interesting to them)
- Frequently misspelled words
- "Trash" words (familiar words that students agree not to use, such as *walked, said, talked, good,* and *nice,* in order to use more varied alternatives)
- "Recycled" words (alternative words to use instead of familiar options, such as *garrulous* instead of *talkative*)
- Color-coded word walls (for example, color code verbs, nouns, and adjectives to help students find parts of speech easily)
- Tier two words
- Hallway word walls (extend word learning into the school hallways)

In addition to traditional word walls, digital word walls can support and enhance concept development and your word-learning goals as well. These two digital tools will get you started. Visit **go.SolutionTree.com/literacy** for live links to these resources.

1. Padlet (https://padlet.com) is an online space to create a collaborative, digital word wall. With one click, users can create sticky notes that can include text, images, links, and videos. Padlet is a useful, collaborative tool and can serve as an online reference space to collect key vocabulary for content units, a place to include links to additional resources, and much more. For example, let's say a teacher is teaching a unit of study on the topic of volcanoes. She uses the online Padlet bulletin board to record virtual sticky notes, with key vocabulary such as *lava, eruption, mantle,* and *tectonic plates.* On each note, she includes a definition as well as an image or link to a video that provides a nonlinguistic representation of the term. In addition, on another sticky note, she records links to additional online resources and websites that students may explore. Using this virtual bulletin board, students can independently explore and expand their vocabulary and concept knowledge specific to volcanoes.

2. ThingLink (www.thinglink.com) is a tool that allows teachers and students to make images interactive. As an online tool, it is quite useful for expanding students' understanding, vocabulary, and general knowledge for identified topics. To use it, simply upload an image; identify what ThingLink calls *hotspots,* or areas of interest, on specific parts of the image; and add informational text or web links. In the classroom, teachers can use ThingLink to launch a unit and introduce students to key vocabulary, or ask students to design interactive images as they become more familiar with a topic. For example, a primary teacher may be introducing students to polar bears in an Arctic unit of study. She selects and uploads an image of a polar bear to her class website. On the image of the polar bear, she identifies hotspots where students can click to learn more information. One hotspot, for example, includes a BBC video featuring additional information specific to polar bear cubs. Another hotspot links to KidZone (www.kidzone.ws) where students can read and learn additional facts and interesting information about polar bears. Still another link connects students to a National Geographic live camera that tracks polar bear activity in Churchill, Manitoba. Using this interactive image, students quickly broaden their understanding and vocabulary around polar bears and their habitat by viewing, listening to, and reading more about them.

Need a few more ideas? *Top Tips for Word Walls* (Tyson, n.d.b), downloaded by thousands of educators, includes several ideas from Garden City Elementary School to help get your creative juices flowing. Visit **go.SolutionTree.com/literacy** for a live link to this resource.

Step 4: Add Images to Accompany Words

When observing classrooms with word walls, we usually see an alphabetical display of words on cards. Nonlinguistic word walls are the exception, not the rule. As the saying goes, "A picture is worth a thousand words." Encourage students to create images or find pictures and symbols to accompany each word. Pictographs and images go a long way toward cementing the word meaning.

Representing words by using visuals and pictographs—the third step in Marzano's six-step vocabulary process—appears to have the most impact on student mastery of new words. According to Marzano (2009), the third step is critical and shouldn't be ignored. Achievement soars when students add a pictograph, use a visual, or act out a new word, thus binding the nonlinguistic image to the linguistic definition.

Step 5: Review and Play Games

Reviewing and playing games involving your word walls will help ensure they remain an integral part of instruction and a resource for students—not just part of the scenery. One way to do this is by simply referring to the words on your word walls as you teach and have conversations throughout the school day. Depending on the age of your students, have them practice the spelling by air writing or "writing" the word on their hand with the opposite index finger.

Multiple exposures to new words is key to understanding the nuances of a word's meaning. You can provide multiple exposures as you review words with students and continually use them in new and varied contexts. Have students use words verbally with a partner or in a small group. Use digital tools, such as those discussed in depth in appendix A (page 107), to vary these exposures and extend opportunities for review. Kahoot!, for example, could be used for periodic review or quizzing.

In addition to these methods, there are countless specific activities and games for reviewing word wall vocabulary. Word jars, Connect a Word, and Save the Last Word for Me, which we describe in the following sections, are just a few examples of engaging ways to review vocabulary. Kimberly has compiled more than twenty additional varied word wall activities, games, and fun ideas for reviewing words with primary and intermediate students (see Tyson, n.d.a; visit **go.SolutionTree.com/literacy** for a live link to this resource). Additionally, we recommend *Vocabulary Games for the Classroom*, a professional resource by Lindsay Carleton and Robert J. Marzano (2010), which includes many game-like activities that reinforce words and help students play with words while adding to their understanding of new vocabulary.

Word Jars

An engaging way to involve word walls during instruction is to make *word jars* to keep a tally of how frequently students use new vocabulary. Each time a student or the teacher correctly uses a word found on a word wall, that person adds a piece of candy or a cotton ball to the jar. When the jar is full, the class gets a reward, such as a popcorn party, for example. The most important element, of course, is the practice of using new words in oral language. Other, simpler ways to acknowledge students using words are to flick the classroom lights, give a high five, cheer, and so on.

Connect a Word

Another fun way to review a bank of words is through the game Connect a Word. This is meant as a culminating activity related to a specific unit of study at the intermediate level. Say a fifth-grade class has just completed a unit of study related to weather systems. The word wall includes vocabulary terms such as *sun, windchill, sea breeze, land breeze, temperature, precipitation, global wind, jet stream, winds, pressure difference, humidity*, and so on. To prepare, the teacher makes a duplicate set of words from the unit word wall. During class time, she distributes one word card to each student. To begin, a student places his word in the center of the floor and provides a definition. Any student can follow, placing his or her word on the floor next to the first word, and telling the relationship between the two words by using them in a sentence. For example, if the first word was *temperature* and the next student placed the word *windchill* next to it, he might say something like, "*Windchill* is when the air *temperature* feels cooler on the skin than the actual *temperature*." At will, the next student places a word card on the floor touching either *temperature* or *windchill* and so on. Connect a Word creates a fun way to review words and build language. In addition, it also helps students think deeply about relationships between words and provides a vehicle for them to practice shifting word knowledge from their receptive to expressive vocabulary.

Save the Last Word for Me

Save the Last Word for Me (Beers, 2003) is a game appropriate for students at the upper elementary level. Its clearly defined structure is perfect for reviewing vocabulary and helping students transition to using new words. The strategy promotes and extends deeper understanding of academic vocabulary since it requires students to participate actively as speakers and listeners. The strategy is best used prior to a quiz or test to help students practice and review vocabulary related to a unit of study.

Consider the following steps for this game.

- Print multiple sets of vocabulary terms with a word on one side and the definition on the reverse side (one set for each group).
- Print the directions for each group (see the reproducible "Save the Last Word for Me Directions" on page 70).
- Place the printed directions and terms in a plastic bag or sleeve for each group of students.
- Divide students into groups of three to five. It's important that groups are small, so students have the opportunity to participate and discuss.

To begin, one student draws a card from the deck and another student defines the term. Moving around the circle, each student adds to the definition, refining and adding examples along the way. The person who drew the card gets the last word and can add to the definition or revise it before students agree on a definition.

Students take turns drawing cards. If students don't know a specific term or concept, they can agree to use the text, a glossary, or an online dictionary to gain clarity. The goal is for students to review and deepen understanding of concepts and specific terms, so making sure they clarify their thinking is important. Even though low tech, Save the Last Word for Me serves as an interactive, engaging way to review and extend word learning well suited to academic vocabulary found within content texts.

Anchored Word Learning

Anchored word learning, a strategy originally developed by Beck and colleagues (2013), is ideal to use with elementary students when read-alouds are typically part of the daily routine. It provides a strong and meaningful context for introducing vocabulary. By using the power of read-alouds to introduce targeted words within context, this strategy has the power to enrich and expand the vocabulary of young students by anchoring tier two vocabulary to context and conversation.

Trade books and picture books provide excellent sources of higher-level, sophisticated words important for expanding vocabulary. They frequently expose students to words that they would not typically see in leveled books. According to Beck's figures, if teachers read aloud once a day, students are exposed to an additional 540 words a year, and for those teachers who read aloud twice each day, students are introduced to more than 1,000 additional words in the span of a school year. This is a perfect example of how to create exposure and provide incidental word-learning opportunities.

Beck and colleagues (2013) suggest selecting three tier two words each time you read aloud. Tier two words, as we discussed at length previously, are high-utility, cross-content words. This means that you should carefully select words from each read-aloud that you deem useful in many contexts. With little preparation and little additional time, teachers can easily incorporate the anchored word-learning strategy into everyday read-alouds. See appendix B (page 121) for a list of texts containing suggested tier two vocabulary words for primary and intermediate grades.

Prior to an anchored word-learning exercise, you should complete three simple preparation steps, which take around five minutes.

1. **Select a read-aloud:** Choose from books by favorite authors, recommended books, new books, old favorites, and picture and trade books.
2. **Identify three words for instruction:** As you preview the book or chapter, select three tier two words that will expand students' vocabulary and will likely appear in varied contexts.
3. **Mark the three words with a sticky note the first time each appears in text:** This actually has two steps embedded. First, place a sticky note on the pages where each word appears. Next, write the three words on a separate sticky note, and place this note inside the front cover of the book. That way, it serves as a reminder of the targeted words when you reread the book the following year. Doing both of these things saves valuable prep time in future years.

An anchored word-learning exercise itself entails five steps, which we summarize here (Tyson, 2012c).

1. **Read words in context:** Read each targeted word in context, and briefly bring attention to it. It is very important for students to hear a complete, fluent reading of the entire text first. Do not engage in lengthy discussion of any of the words as you read aloud.

2. **Teach spelling and sound:** Have students repeat each word aloud. Write the word on a sentence strip, saying the letters aloud as you write the word. Have students voice anything they notice that is unusual about the spelling, such as double letters, a silent *E*, and so forth. Have young students air write the word while saying each letter aloud. Older students can spell the word with their hand by forming each letter on the palm of the opposite hand or tracing letters on their desks.

3. **Provide the meaning:** Reread the words in context, and provide the meaning of each with a student-friendly definition.

4. **Give extended examples:** Provide examples for each word beyond the context of the story. Encourage students to provide examples of their own so they personalize the word, relating it to their own context.

5. **Create a read-aloud word wall:** To create a simple way to review words and provide an opportunity for multiple exposures, create a community word wall featuring words specifically found in read-alouds.

Plan to periodically revisit the words. When students have mastered each word, you can then move it to the class word wall.

We love the read-aloud word wall and its ability to serve as a visual reminder of words and their spellings, as well as a means for reviewing words. But providing varied opportunities for students to revisit and review words is essential, particularly for native speakers who have gaps in their vocabulary and English learners. We encourage teachers to incorporate words from read-alouds into digital review tools such as Flashcard Stash (http://flashcardstash.com) where students can hear the words again within context. Customizing word lists is easy to do, provides an additional opportunity for students to see and hear words, and serves as a check for understanding.

Recap

We know that many students enter primary classrooms word poor, often due to a lack of opportunities to hear a rich variety of words. Vocabulary development plays a critical role in success as elementary students learn to read and comprehend text. Selecting words strategically along with teaching those words through direct instruction, wordplay, and reading aloud helps build these students' receptive and expressive vocabularies. Digital tools and apps can provide opportunities for elementary students to hear words pronounced, see images related to specific words, review vocabulary in a game-like setting, and create collaborative word walls with other students. The variety of linguistic and nonlinguistic strategies, word wall activities, and games presented in this chapter will go a long way toward enriching the experience students have with words and preparing them for academic success.

Digital Tools for Elementary Students

Flashcard Stash (http://flashcardstash.com): Games and review
Free Rice (www.freerice.com): Games and review
Padlet (https://padlet.com): Digital word wall
Popplet (https://popplet.com): Concept map tool
Shahi (http://blachan.com/shahi): Visual dictionary
ThingLink (www.thinglink.com): Images with key vocabulary

NEXT STEPS

Consider the following questions individually or discuss them with colleagues or in literacy leadership team settings.

Teachers

- Think about how you currently teach vocabulary to your elementary students. How do you incorporate rich opportunities with words both linguistically and nonlinguistically?
- Select one linguistic and one nonlinguistic strategy from this chapter. Get to know each well, perhaps practicing with a grade-level team member. Think about how to use the strategy to support a unit of study, and try it out. Provide feedback to a team member. Would you change anything the next time you try it? What worked? Perhaps more important, what didn't?
- Check out the ideas for word walls in this chapter and in the Teacher Toolkit on Kimberly's website (Tyson, 2013g). Visit **go.SolutionTree.com /literacy** for a live link to this resource. Think about developing a new word wall in your classroom. How will you use it? Reflect on how you will keep it active, growing, and integrated into instructional activities.
- Share the five steps for making word walls with a colleague. How did these easy-to-follow steps move your thinking or nudge your practice?
- Do you currently incorporate digital tools and apps into word learning and practice? Take time to preview several that would support your vocabulary goals (for example, direct instruction, practice, review, and building word consciousness). Determine which digital tools best support your goals, and begin integrating them into instruction and independent learning activities.

Literacy Leadership Teams

- What guidelines, if any, have you given to colleagues for word walls? What are you now considering adding or changing?

- How could your school incorporate word walls into unexpected places such as the gymnasium, cafeteria, and hallways? What kind of words would you feature?
- How might you model the use of motor imaging, concept circles, or word wheels in a staff meeting or professional learning session?
- How do the strategies included in this chapter help build your teachers' toolbox of effective vocabulary strategies? What can you, as a literacy leadership team member, do to support implementation?
- Do teachers currently incorporate digital tools and apps into word learning and practice? Take time to preview several that would support vocabulary goals in your school (for example, direct instruction, practice, review, and building word consciousness). Model a few digital tools in a staff meeting. Provide time for teachers to check them out and determine which best support their vocabulary goals.
- Encourage teachers to create an online shared space in Evernote or OneNote, Google Docs, or a Pinterest board where teachers can share resources, lesson plans, images, and word wall ideas with one another.

Save the Last Word for Me Directions

One student selects a card from the deck of terms and shares the term with the other members in the group.

On a piece of paper, each student jots down what he or she knows about the term. (This can also be in one's head, with each student thinking about what he or she knows about the meaning of the term.)

When they are finished, each student takes a turn sharing his or her reflections and responses. As each participant shares his or her thoughts, other students can share their own thoughts and responses.

The student who drew the card gets the last word by sharing his or her reflections and reactions or by stating a fresh view if the responses of others have altered his or her original thinking about the term. If students are unsure, they can refer to the text or handouts for clarification.

Next, another student draws a new card, and the process repeats.

CHAPTER 6

Vocabulary Strategies for Secondary Students

As students progress into middle and high school, they are bombarded with increasingly complex content and the copious domain-specific vocabulary that accompanies it. Students sit in as many as seven classes per day and face the varying expectations of all those teachers. In middle school, students undergo vast physical and emotional changes, and in high school, many engage in extracurricular activities, work part-time jobs, and enjoy active social lives. For secondary students, the heaviest vocabulary load looms over them while they are at their most disinterested and least supervised.

Older students also provide us with a great opportunity. If we can interest them in acquiring academic vocabulary—or if we can capitalize on an interest already cultivated—they can enter postsecondary education or the workplace with an advantage over many of their peers. William E. Nagy and Patricia A. Herman (1987) estimate that typical students enter kindergarten with vocabularies of five thousand to ten thousand words and graduate with vocabularies of about fifty thousand words. With the increased rigor of new state and provincial standards, we can reasonably infer that high school graduates should consider the fifty-thousand-word mark as a floor and not a ceiling. Beck et al. (2013) estimate that seniors near the top of their class know four times as many words as their lower-performing peers, and, tragically, that high-performing third graders know as many words as low-performing seniors. If the lowest quartile of seniors in every graduating class has a vocabulary equivalent to an advanced third grader's, we should all be concerned about the literacy skills of our youth.

Scott Greenwood (2004) notes, "There is a great divide between what we know about vocabulary instruction and what we (often, still) do" (p. 28). We have learned much in the 20th and 21st centuries about effective vocabulary instruction, yet it appears that little has trickled down to impact everyday instruction. There seems to be a definite gap between what research suggests and what teachers actually do specific to vocabulary instruction.

Secondary teachers of all subjects understand the importance of discipline-specific vocabulary; however, many of them have concerns about teaching it effectively. Today, many digital textbooks, including web-based text, support word learning by including hyperlinked definitions, pronunciations of specific words, translations, and interactive graphics and illustrations. But it's still difficult to decide where to begin. Too often, teachers rely on rote methods that mirror how they were taught. Many have tried the following strategies: preteaching the vocabulary of a new unit or chapter; providing simplistic synonyms for important terms; directing students to use footnotes or the textbook's glossary when they need support; and using word walls. While these strategies are certainly helpful for students, they may not be robust enough to allow them to become independent vocabulary problem solvers. It requires far more than words displayed on a wall to help older students tackle all the unfamiliar vocabulary they will encounter in complex texts in the various disciplines.

We designed the ideas and strategies that follow to enhance the vocabulary instruction that you're already delivering in your classroom. We tailored them for older students. They appear in three general categories: (1) strategies using nonlinguistic representations, (2) strategies using collaboration, and (3) strategies for independent processing. These three categories, while not exhaustive, seem to be the categories into which many effective secondary strategies fall. It is important to keep in mind that when selecting any strategy, your instructional purpose should be front and center. Also, remember that some strategies work better with certain types of content or within certain disciplines. At times, simpler is better. You will see that each recommended strategy includes information about how and when to best apply it, and to what content.

Strategies Using Nonlinguistic Representations

Many vocabulary strategies that include some sort of nonlinguistic image or demonstration (like a graphic, symbol, sketch, visualization, or movement) have become popular, and for good reason—they work better than saying, "Look it up in the dictionary." This section of strategies suggests ways to use nonlinguistic representations as part of word learning for secondary students.

Revised Frayer Model

Dorothy Ann Frayer, Wayne C. Fredrick, and Herbert John Klausmeier (1969) developed what researchers now typically refer to as the Frayer model. It is a strategy that uses a graphic organizer to support the learning of conceptual vocabulary. This technique requires students to define the target word you provide, differentiate it from other terms by naming critical attributes, and generate examples and nonexamples. Students place this information on a chart with four squares with the target word in the center (see figure 6.1).

Many teachers with whom we have worked over the years have used (and misused!) the Frayer model visual we provide in figure 6.1. Handing students ten or twenty copies of the organizer and asking them to apply it to a list of vocabulary words is *not* the way it was intended to be used, though we have seen well-intentioned teachers employ it this

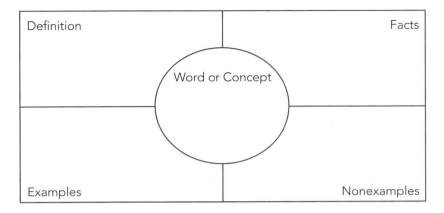

Figure 6.1: Frayer model chart.

way without anticipating the possibility of creating Frayer model overload in their classes by using the strategy far too frequently. We have also seen an entire class using the Frayer model graphic in a whole-group discussion format, spending an inordinate amount of time with it, focusing on a nonconceptual word like a specific historical figure or a narrowly defined term. In contrast, the model—when used as intended—should highlight words that pack some definitional heft. In other words, these words should generate a robust discussion of nonexamples in particular so that the learner can understand the fine line that separates the term in question from other terms, especially those that are similar.

We propose a modification to the basic Frayer model graphic and strategy to include the power of a nonlinguistic image. Figure 6.2 (page 74) illustrates these modifications in a graphic organizer that contains the following components.

- A definition (ideally, a student-friendly one)
- The defining characteristics or critical attributes
- The word itself (ideally written very large, also to enhance memory)
- Examples
- A visual
- Nonexamples

Generating the examples and a visual *before* discussing nonexamples can help students seek to solidify their conceptual understanding. Frayer and her colleagues (1969) certainly didn't intend for students (and teachers) to struggle with discussing nonexamples, but teachers and students have told us that spending more time on the positives—meaning what the term actually *is* versus what it *is not*—leads to a fruitful discussion, prevents stalling, and lessens frustration. Charlene Cobb and Camille Blachowicz (2014) recommend a modification they call a *Frayer Model Word Square*, which includes the visual component that we also recommend. However, in our graphic organizer for the revised Frayer model, we believe the cross-out feature for nonexamples provides additional visual support to help learners better distinguish the features that make something an example versus a nonexample. We also like to work from a definition to the essential attributes or characteristics, indicated by the arrow in our graphic organizer.

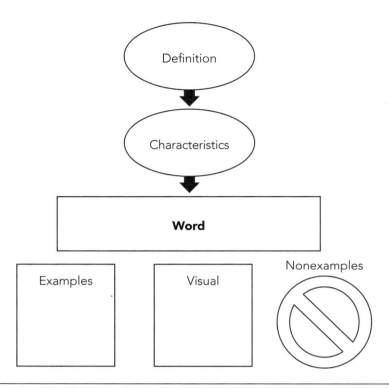

Figure 6.2: Modified Frayer model graphic organizer.

Sometimes a helpful way to think of nonexamples is to contrast them with examples. Students can often readily supply answers to the question, What does the term remind me of? However, the question, What does the term *not* remind me of? can help students think about nonexamples. You may also want to try the question, What might be the opposite of what it reminds me of? Talking about nonexamples should help students understand the finer points of what makes something an example and what separates it from a nonexample; the idea is not to struggle unproductively. In other words, if you can't generate a long list of nonexamples, fine—go back to examples and generate more ideas there instead.

Circling back to intentionality, we recommend thinking first about your instructional purpose and saving the revised Frayer model for when you really need to pack a punch. Teachers should choose to apply the Frayer model to words that students need to learn deeply and well and those that are worthy of such careful consideration. This usually means that they reflect conceptual knowledge important within the discipline being studied—not just declarative knowledge.

English Language Arts Example

Let's walk through how you might use the modified organizer. First, the choice of the term is important. We would not choose a term like *soliloquy*, because it's not rich enough conceptually to take valuable class time for students to engage in a discussion of it separate from the context of any particular soliloquy. *Soliloquy* has a specific, unquestionable definition, and there are plenty of examples in the world of drama. Generating nonexamples would not be a good use of time, either, because there are so many literary terms that are pertinent to plays, and so few dramatic conventions that are similar enough to be confused with a soliloquy. We could say that *dialogue* is a nonexample, but where would we go from there? Perhaps *monologue*? And then would students be confused between *soliloquy* and *monologue* because both are often lengthy, and both are delivered by one performer? A teacher would not want to spend a lot of time on this area with novice learners, like freshmen who are tackling Shakespeare for perhaps the first time.

Let's take a simpler literary term, *theme*. This term is incredibly complicated for elementary students to understand, and secondary students who are weak readers continue to have problems with it. Working with students in a whole-group fashion, we might first ask them how they would define the term and then mediate the group toward a definition like this one: "a deep, overall idea of a literary work that we gain from analyzing details of plot, character, and author's purpose."

Next, we would move to the defining attributes of *theme*. We would point out that a literary work does not overtly state the theme (unlike a moral, which could go into the nonexamples portion of our organizer if a student offered it during this part of the discussion). In addition, we would record the idea that a theme is a complete idea, stated in a sentence—not just a topic like betrayal or love and not an aphorism like "To err is human, to forgive divine." These represent common misconceptions students have.

In the examples section of the organizer, we work with students to create theme statements from recent literary works we have studied. If that turns out to be too difficult, we could start with more familiar works such as nursery rhymes, familiar children's books, or classic movies like *The Wizard of Oz* (LeRoy & Fleming, 1939) or *How the Grinch Stole Christmas!* (Jones & Washam, 1966). Most students can state themes from childhood stories or movies that they have repeated exposure to. This kind of scaffolded discussion is helpful as we move on to stating themes for some of the literature we have studied in class.

For a visual, a sketch of an open book with a big question mark above it might work, or we could write the words *the message* above the sketch of the book. Of course, teachers could also take student suggestions or allow several students to show a sketch they would use if they were doing the activity independently.

For nonexamples, we may include *topic*, *main or central idea*, *moral*, and *author's purpose* at a minimum. We would need to review what all these terms mean as we place them in the nonexamples section. They are all somewhat related to *theme*, yet they are *not* exactly the same—this is the critical difference students must discern.

Mathematics Example

Now let's walk through a mathematics example with the revised Frayer model. In middle school and early in high school, one term that may deserve a deep discussion is the term *equation*. A definition for *equation* might be "a mathematical statement that the values of two expressions are equal." This definition is important because it uses the term *values*, which is more specific than words students might first offer up, like *things*.

The characteristics portion of the discussion (and of the organizer) should generate some stimulating conversation. An *equation* contains an equal sign. It also may have at least one *variable*. As noted in the definition, it has two *expressions*. All of these are important domain-specific terms that should arise as students participate in the dialogue the teacher facilitates. If they don't come up, you need to guide students to the correct use of the terms through your cues and questioning. You may also want students to articulate that any mathematical operation applied to one side of the equation must also be applied to the other because of the concept of equal values on either side of the equal sign.

In the examples section of the organizer, you may want to generate one-step and two-step equations, equations with fractions, equations with decimals, and so on—whatever reflects the current learning of your class.

For a visual, encourage students to think symbolically about what an equation represents. I might sketch a seesaw with two people on it, but equally balanced, or an image of scales that are evenly balanced, perhaps with all sorts of digits piled onto each tray. Urge students to envision other similar analogies and what the accompanying visuals might be.

Lastly, in the nonexamples portion of the chart, you'd at least want students to generate an expression (and to be able to explain why one expression does not an equation make). An inequality is also not an equation, and if they are familiar with inequalities, then this term should appear there as well.

TIP Chart

The TIP acronym stands for *term, information, picture*. Basically, a TIP chart (Rollins, 2014) is a three-column poster displayed so students can quickly use it to remind themselves of the meaning of an important content-area word. In essence, it's a vocabulary anchor chart. Unlike the original or revised Frayer model, the TIP chart is useful for words that are fairly straightforward in meaning—not ones with heavy conceptual weight. A completed TIP chart should serve as an at-a-glance reference for important disciplinary words, and teachers must keep this overarching purpose in mind if the strategy is to be most beneficial.

The teacher can first model how to create the three columns, and later, involve the entire class in deciding what information to record and what picture to draw to go with each word. A TIP chart in poster form should remain visible during an entire chapter or unit and can also reappear when it's time to review for standardized tests or a final exam.

The best time to use the TIP chart strategy is when beginning a new section of instruction, like a chapter or unit. To begin, draw the headings and columns as shown in figure 6.3 on chart paper or a whiteboard. The chart should be ready when you're introducing the unit.

Term	Information	Picture

Figure 6.3: Blank TIP chart.

With the chart ready, announce the first word, and call students' attention to the importance of this word in the current segment of instruction. Write the word in the Term column. Then share the formal and full definition, which ideally would also be printed in the text or on a screen or board in the classroom. Along with students, develop a short, student-friendly definition or a brief list to record in the Information column. Do *not* write the full, formal definition in column two. Lastly, provide or co-create a simple visual in the Picture column.

So, for the term *soliloquy* in English class, we would give the formal definition: "a long, usually serious speech that a character in a play makes to an audience and that reveals the character's thoughts" (Soliloquy, n.d.). We might talk for a minute about the fact that playwrights use soliloquies to help the audience understand what a character is thinking. So, in the middle column, we might write "when someone in the play thinks out loud." And, to emphasize the fact that a character usually gives this kind of speech alone on the stage, we might draw a single stick figure with lines emanating from its face to indicate that he or she is speaking (see figure 6.4).

Term	Information	Picture
Soliloquy	When someone in the play thinks out loud	

Figure 6.4: TIP chart example.

As another example, for the term *monopoly*, the full definition might be "the exclusive possession or control of the supply or trade in a commodity or service." We assume that the teacher is also teaching the term *commodity* along with *monopoly*. In the second column for *monopoly*, the teacher may write "control of a product or service." In the third column, he or she might draw a large square that surrounds smaller squares, thus showing the dominance of the one provider. Students might also suggest something that symbolizes a monopoly to them, like some kind of smartphone surrounded by other types of cell phones, but with the phone appearing much larger or more prominent, or with the other phones crossed out.

Teachers can gradually do less and less with TIP charts and encourage students to create their own in their physical notebooks or record them in digital notebooks such as LiveBinders or OneNote. As we mentioned previously, students can share pages or notebooks within both of these online platforms. Thus, they can share examples with one another or collaborate when making a TIP chart so that if any individual is confused about a word, he or she can get ideas from others. They can preview the first part of each chapter or unit (in any class) and try to complete a personal TIP chart to keep in their organizational system. Students can use this portable strategy with any content area and any textbook throughout secondary school and well into college. Most textbooks call the reader's attention to important terminology by listing it at the beginning of a section or chapter or by formatting words in bold. These are great candidates for a TIP chart.

Word Scales

Angela has used word scales with middle school and high school teachers as they attempt to bring more attention to specific vocabulary—words of a general nature in addition to words specific to a discipline. The visual for a word scale is a simple diagonal line drawn from the bottom left of a surface to the top right, with an arrow tip at the top, denoting directionality. It supports learning sets of words that are similar in meaning but that differ in either intensity or sophistication. For example, if we list words that are about warmth or heat, we might start at the bottom left with the word *warm*, and then ask, "What's a word that would mean a little higher temperature than warm?" Students might offer words like *warmer* and *comfortable*, which would both be fine. But if they offered words like *hot* or *toasty*, the teacher would need to move them up higher toward the arrow point, because the connotation of those words is of a higher temperature than just the word *warm*. We might continue, and if students could not continue generating more intense words than *mild, lukewarm, cozy,* or *hot*, we would want to suggest *temperate, snug, heated, balmy, roasting,* and *scorching*. This particular example depicts using general academic words and pushing students toward greater accuracy along with greater specificity.

Word scales can accommodate some content-specific words. In a social studies example, students who study different types of communities at various grade levels may encounter unfamiliar words, at least in terms of the specific meanings of those words as they relate to size or governance. Figure 6.5 shows the word scale that one middle school teacher collaborated with her students to make in order to clarify some of these words and their relationships.

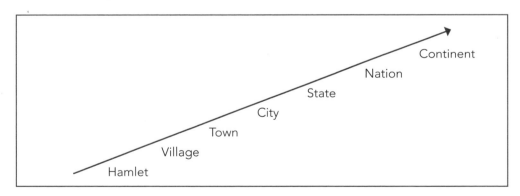

Figure 6.5: Word scale example.

Angela supported teachers in seventh-grade mathematics classes as students worked with the geometric concept of angles. At certain points in each of the lessons, it seemed that students were a bit confused about terms like *supplementary, complementary, acute,* and *obtuse*. In reflecting on the lesson, Angela recommended that teachers consider using a word scale with the specific terms from the smallest in degrees to the largest: *acute, right, obtuse, straight*.

While the concepts of *supplementary* and *complementary* deal with pairs of angles and how each angle relates to another, which is quite different from ranking a single angle along a scale by its number of degrees, if the students could clarify the four measurement terms Angela suggested, she felt they could then deal with other terminology more easily.

Strategies Using Collaboration

Often when students get to talk with each other, they instantly perk up. Most of them love an opportunity to stop focusing on the teacher and start engaging with their peers. These strategies allow for meaningful conversation among students about words they need to know to succeed.

Word Knowledge Through Questioning

In this strategy, students must have a working knowledge of some words that are critical to the current segment of instruction. Word knowledge through questioning (Allen, 2014) won't work if they don't have at least a basic understanding of the words you select. However, this strategy is flexible enough to work well with both tier two and tier three words.

To implement this strategy, place the students in groups. You may want to display all the words you are using on a poster, a whiteboard, or a word wall. Provide each group with questions about how the important terms relate to each other. (Each group can have the same questions, or you can differentiate the questions to align with each group's current expertise.)

For example, in a unit on genetics, a teacher might ask, "How are *alleles* and *inherited traits* related? How are *autosome*, *chromosome*, and *dominant* related?" Teachers can select two or three words for each question, and, if desired, offer advanced or challenge questions that ask students to discuss pairs of words and their relationship to other pairs of words. In a study of forms of government, a teacher might ask, "How is the relationship of an absolute monarchy to a constitutional monarchy like or unlike the relationship of a true democracy to a representative democracy? Provide examples to add to your explanation." In mathematics, a teacher might ask, "How is the relationship between a fraction and division like or unlike the relationship between a base and an exponent?" These challenge questions are an excellent way to keep higher-performing students engaged and can ignite an interesting conversation among all learners. All of these examples also require students to have deep knowledge of the content.

Allow the groups to work and discuss the questions for a while. Then, have groups report out and question each other, or you can move to a more traditional whole-class discussion with all groups adding to the conversation. This strategy is valuable in that by listening to students' discussions, you can hear and correct any misunderstandings immediately.

Because this strategy allows for collaboration, students are likely to be more engaged and want to do the work. Because the questions often lead to more divergent answers, students who are often reticent about participating for fear of being wrong enjoy it as well.

Jigsaw Vocabulary

Many teachers are familiar with the jigsaw method that Elliot Aronson and Shelley Patnoe (1997) developed and promoted. Jigsaw is a specific cooperative learning process that both students and teachers can readily learn. It requires no special materials, and teachers can implement it with just about any type or amount of content, but we recommend adapting it specially to a fairly large number of general academic words or domain-specific terms. It can serve as an excellent way to initially teach words or to review them before an important assessment.

To use the jigsaw strategy with vocabulary learning, first compile a list of words you want to use. This could be a set of words from a chapter or unit or a large number of words that have been important in your class over time. Angela used the strategy with eighth-grade students at the end of the school year as they prepared to take a high school placement exam that would determine which English course they would take, narrowing the list of all possible terms they might encounter on the vocabulary section of the test to seventy-five words.

The second step in a traditional jigsaw activity is breaking the content up into manageable chunks, which students handle in cooperative groups of four to six. In the original jigsaw strategy, all teams work on the same content in two groups—a *home* group and an *expert* group (which further divides the total content in portions for individuals within the group). In jigsaw vocabulary, you can use this traditional method of dividing the content, or, if you have a large number of words (as Angela and her eighth graders did), you may need to adapt this exercise and assign different groups to different content. Angela divided the class into five groups and assigned each group fifteen words. Figure 6.6 represents the two methods of dividing content and depicts four cooperative groups with four members each.

1. Traditional method

All groups in the class have the same content.

Each group divides the content with each person taking a section of the whole.

Individuals meet with others who are experts in the same section.

2. Adapted method

All groups have different content.

Each group divides the content as directed or as they determine.

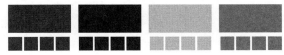

Each person works individually on his or her assigned content.

Figure 6.6: Traditional and adapted jigsaw methods.

After you have chosen which strategy you will use to divide students, you begin to orchestrate the work. If the students have little experience with jigsaws or other cooperative groupings, you will need to appoint the leaders of the home groups so that the work will flow more smoothly. Use your best judgment to form productive groups and to assign effective leaders.

To proceed, students meet in their home groups first and then divide out into their jigsaw pieces. In the traditional method, individuals study their assigned sections and, after a period of time specified by the teacher, meet with others who have the same section. In jigsaw vocabulary activities, students work alone because there aren't others who were assigned the same words. Therefore, in the adaptation, the teacher must be diligent in supporting the individuals as they work independently on their word lists.

The group work might last more than one class period, and if so, you'll need to decide when the individuals rejoin their home groups in order to complete the next step, which is teaching the assigned individual portions. You may also have to create a note-taking template or other handout to support the group members as they take part in the instruction that each peer provides in this step.

In the adapted method, you need to orchestrate whole-class discussion of all the words to expose the whole class to the entire set of words. When Angela used the adapted method, each group's collection of about fifteen words became the focus of a fifteen-minute segment at the beginning of each seventy-minute class for a couple of weeks prior to the placement exam. They added any words not covered one day to the next day, but they discussed most of the words very quickly, with the individuals who had been assigned the words taking the lead in teaching. For some words, Angela encouraged students to pantomime or somehow act out the meaning to make the content particularly memorable. Students enjoyed the challenge of creating a dramatic visual representation, and in many cases, this twenty-second action sealed the meanings of certain words into classmates' minds.

Remember, however, that jigsaw should turn most of the responsibility for the learning over to the students. The strategy won't be effective if you follow it or replace it with lengthy, teacher-led instruction. That's why actively monitoring throughout the process is critical. In the adapted method we described here, brevity and meaningfulness are also important. Some of the best-remembered words are the ones for which a student (not the teacher) provided a powerful synonym, example, or dramatic interpretation.

After the entire process is completed, following up with some type of individual assessment to check retention of the material may provide useful information to you and each student. You could choose something as informal as the digital tool Padlet to use as an exit ticket or something as formal as a test. Students quickly see that jigsaw sessions, even though high-energy and enjoyable, are not just fun and games. They are excellent learning opportunities.

Save the Last Word for Me

Save the Last Word for Me (Beers, 2003), first introduced in this book in chapter 5, is an ideal strategy to foster interaction, increase levels of engagement, and promote deeper processing of vocabulary and content. The strategy requires all students to participate as active speakers and listeners. Its clearly defined structure uses a bag containing a deck of cards with vocabulary terms printed on each and asks students to draw a card, reflect on their knowledge of the term, and then discuss in small groups. It's perfect for reviewing vocabulary and gaining deeper understanding of specific terms and content.

It is fairly typical for secondary teachers to provide guided review activities before an exam. Let's say the unit includes about twenty-five terms that students must recognize and understand how to use correctly within context. Save the Last Word for Me serves as an engaging vehicle for students to practice doing so. As we noted in the last chapter, you can use this activity with upper elementary students as well as secondary students. See chapter 5 (page 65) for the steps for implementing this activity, and see the reproducible "Save the Last Word for Me Directions" (page 70) for detailed directions.

Save the Last Word for Me is not only a great review tool but also a good strategy for students to practice using terms in an authentic context. In addition, students can use an Alphabox template (see the following section beginning on page 83 for more on Alphaboxes) to record all the terms or only the terms they missed and need to review before the quiz or test.

Sometimes, if the bank of terms is large (as is more often the case with secondary students), we suggest simply printing one master deck of cards and placing about six cards in each bag. After a few minutes, signal the groups to trade bags of terms, and in so doing, each group will have new terms to review. In this way, groups focus on a limited number of terms to review, and the task doesn't overwhelm them.

While Save the Last Word for Me is low tech, sometimes simpler is better. It delivers by supporting interaction and engagement, deeper conversations, and higher-level processing. Kimberly has used it frequently with students and teachers for professional learning, and she's never been disappointed.

Alphaboxes

The Alphabox, as developed by Linda Hoyt (2009), is an excellent strategy for activating prior knowledge and building vocabulary and comprehension before, during, and after reading. Alphaboxes elicit conversations that help students make connections to new vocabulary they will encounter and aid comprehension. It is an ideal strategy for helping students organize and learn the academic vocabulary found in informational text. Although the tool is simple, the discussion that occurs when using this tool is often lively and ideal for building background knowledge. While it's a straightforward graphic organizer, teachers can use an Alphabox template in a variety of ways to build vocabulary and comprehension.

To implement this strategy, announce the topic or concept prior to reading or discussion, and ask students to brainstorm terms that connect to the topic. As students mention words related to the topic, you record each term on a chart or whiteboard in the appropriate space on the alphabet grid, each term starting with the letter denoted (see figure 6.7). You may also record the definitions here if desired. Each time you add a word, briefly discuss with students the meaning of the word and how it relates to the topic. Prior to reading, you can add specific key words that may be unfamiliar to students but that are critical to understanding the text. After reading, you can include additional terms as well.

Alphaboxes

A	B	C	D
E	F	G	H
I	J	K	L
M	N	O	P
Q	R	S	T
U	V	W	X, Y, Z

Figure 6.7: Alphaboxes template.

For example, when beginning a unit on volcanoes with sixth-grade students, Kimberly introduced the topic and asked students to brainstorm what they already knew about volcanoes and terms associated with them. As students mentioned terms, she recorded them in the corresponding alphabet square on the whiteboard. Students quickly named *lava*, *mantle*, and *Hawaii*. In addition, she added *tectonic plates* and *molten* and provided brief definitions. Following this, students read the text and viewed a short video about volcanoes. After reading, students engaged in a discussion circling back to the terms and added to their understanding of them.

Following are some suggestions for using Alphaboxes (Tyson, 2012a).

- Students should receive individual copies of the Alphabox chart. Then they can independently record and add key terms in the appropriate box as they read the text, participate in a discussion, or view a video. Doing this individualizes and differentiates terms according to each student's learning needs.
- Students can come together in pairs, in small groups, or as a class to discuss specific terms they added to the graphic organizer and any words they now think are irrelevant and should be removed. It is important that, when sharing words, students justify why they included the terms in their Alphabox.
- Small groups share their words with the class and justify the inclusion of any word on their list in relation to its importance or significance to the unit of study.
- As the class comes together to discuss which terms they should include on the class Alphabox organizer, the Alphabox chart becomes a portable, topical word wall. After all, word walls are not just for primary students!
- As a study tool, intermediate and secondary students can use their Alphabox charts individually or in small groups as they review for a quiz or test. Students can also record words in their print or digital vocabulary journals.
- Students can also easily add terms to Alphaboxes using a collaborative space such as Padlet, OneNote, Evernote, or a Google Doc. An online, collaborative version of Alphaboxes also provides students easy access when studying for a quiz or test.

Collaborative Word Walls

Too often, we're stuck thinking that all word walls are limited to displaying sight words in K–2 classrooms. As Janet Allen (1999), author of *Words, Words, Words*, advocates, word walls should be part of every K–12 classroom. With digital technology, creating a collaborative word wall just got easier. Working in small groups, students can jointly develop a word wall using Padlet to support independent research or a unit of study. Not only can they post digital sticky notes with terms, they can also add images, links, and videos to enhance each term or concept. Students can use themed word walls during a collaborative class discussion or access them independently.

In the secondary grades, students tackle many complex and specific words, especially in mathematics, science, and technology classes. Unlike during the elementary years, when words on a word wall might be grouped alphabetically or by some kind of structural similarity (like a spelling pattern), secondary word walls are often best organized thematically or by some sort of classification system. In history classes, category headings could include historical figures, important documents, laws enacted, and conceptual terms, for instance. In mathematics, terms could be grouped by what operation they are closely associated with or with a topic like measurement, data, or problem solving. We recommend that if your word wall gets too crowded, you consider removing or reorganizing some words. Many secondary teachers display only words that go with the current unit of study.

Twitter Hashtags

Twitter (https://twitter.com), a popular social media platform, continually picks up momentum in its number of users; however, many educators have not tapped into its power to support instructional or professional learning goals. As an educational tool, teachers can easily use it to support collaboration. To do so, simply create a hashtag (#) to aggregate and collect students' tweets about a specific topic.

For example, use Twitter to tap background knowledge and to build vocabulary and conceptual understanding specific to World War I, a unit of study in eighth-grade social studies. Using the hashtag #WWITyson (content and teacher's name), you can lead a brainstorming session by having students tweet words or concepts before reading or discussing (similar to Alphaboxes). Students simply add the hashtag to the end of each tweet so the tweets all appear in one stream. In just a few seconds, students can see all the words and concepts their classmates are thinking about related to WWI. Later, as students grow in their understanding, post a word or concept, and ask students to tweet (in 140 characters or fewer) their understanding of that word or concept. We suggest that you post the final tweet encapsulating the definition. Then, students can record the definition in a print or digital notebook or add it to their unit Alphabox sheet. You may discover additional ways to record definitions on these sheets—this is a versatile tool, and teachers can use their best judgment as to what works best for them and their students.

Strategies for Independent Processing

Secondary students must move from being dependent on their teachers to becoming increasingly independent thinkers. They need to learn how they learn best, how they can handle setbacks, and, among other academic skills, how to tackle ongoing vocabulary learning, which becomes increasingly important as they prepare for college and career. The following strategies help support students' independent processing.

Vocabulary Logs

This strategy goes by different names, including *vocabulary journal*, *vocabulary notebook*, and *word log*. While students can use traditional notebooks, digital notebooks such as LiveBinders and OneNote are perfect tools for collecting words as well. Digital notebooks have the advantage of being easily shareable, which can increase opportunities for collaboration. At its core, the notebook—whether print or digital—is a record of student-selected words, their meanings, and their applications. Keeping a personal record of unfamiliar words encountered in text, nonprint media (viewing), and conversation is an engaging assignment that works best in English and social studies classes during segments of instruction without many domain-specific terms. It also works well with independent reading and reinforces the idea that the most memorable learning is self-directed and reflective.

Many teachers have found their way to developing a specific method for implementing vocabulary logs that work well for them and their students. The chart in figure 6.8 features a sample excerpt of the vocabulary log Angela used with her high school students and has shared with secondary teachers all over the United States. The student in this example was in a ninth-grade English class that required him to find at least three new words per week in his independent reading and outside of normal school assignments.

Word	Part of Speech	Context and Source (How was it used when you read, heard, or saw it? Provide enough context for others to understand. Cite your source.)	Definition (in your own words, matching the part of speech)	Application (Write a sentence of your own or use the word in enough context for others to understand the meaning.)
1. Proverbial	Adjective	Found in the *Keynoter* newspaper. "But on the other side of that proverbial coin, do we need a federal document that dictates how the reef will be protected?"	Well-known or typical	I felt like the proverbial third wheel when I went to the park with my best friend and her date.
2. Precursor	Noun	Found in *Sports Afield* magazine. "The oscillating motion was a precursor to a loss of control."	Something that precedes something else happening	The blinking light was a precursor to my enemy's arrival.
3. Exonerate	Verb	Found in the *Sun News* newspaper. "Dexter Jones said that he believed that others were involved in the murder and that a trial might even exonerate Justis Johnson."	To clear of a charge or to free someone from blame	I hope that the true killer is not exonerated and instead pays his debt to society.

Figure 6.8: Sample high school vocabulary log.

*Visit **go.SolutionTree.com/literacy** for a free reproducible version of this figure.*

One middle school teacher created a simplified version of the assignment, as shown in figure 6.9.

Word and Part of Speech	Where You Found It	What It Means in Your Own Words	How to Use It
Traction (noun)	In my silent reading book	It was used differently than I have ever seen before, saying that a person broke his arm and had to be put in traction for six weeks.	I was playing basketball with my friend Harris, and he fell and screamed out in pain. It turned out he had a broken leg and had to be in the hospital in traction for weeks.

Figure 6.9: Sample middle school vocabulary log.

Vocabulary Self-Collection Strategy

The primary purpose of the Vocabulary Self-Collection Strategy (VSS) is to help students generate a list of words to learn based on their prior knowledge and experience with text (Haggard, 1986). This strategy can stimulate word growth and independence as students read text and select vocabulary that they deem important to understanding the content.

In general, VSS includes the following four steps.

1. Selecting the words
2. Defining the words
3. Finalizing the word lists
4. Extending word knowledge

While these four steps are integral to the strategy, they may vary slightly depending upon whether students are working independently or in groups. You can use the strategy to encourage general word learning from students' environments or to support vocabulary learning from text. For example, Kimberly routinely used this strategy to support general word learning with college freshmen. Every week, students collected three words from their environment—listening or reading—that they thought important to learn. For each word, students included the following three pieces of information: (1) the definition of the word, (2) where they heard or read the word, including written context, and (3) why they thought the word was important to learn. The class engaged in a discussion about these words each week. Several students would share their words and their reasons for their importance. Students also recorded their words in a vocabulary notebook. As the semester passed, students were interested to see that (almost magically) they would begin to hear and read the words that were discussed in class. Kimberly found that VSS engaged students in lively discussions and specifically improved word consciousness, a goal of word learning.

Another way that you can implement VSS is to specifically support word acquisition from content text. To do so, you can have students work in cooperative groups and read a chapter from a content text, for example. As they read, they identify words they think they should study and learn to mastery (tier two words). During class discussion, groups share their words and why they think the terms are important to understand the content. Next, the class develops a list of words that includes at least one word from each group. In addition, the teacher can submit a word to the final list and lead an extended discussion and clarify terms.

Another variation of VSS is Vocabulary Self-Collection Strategy Plus (VSS+), developed by classroom researchers (Grisham, Smetana, & Wolsey, 2015). The developers expand upon the basics of VSS and incorporate technology to extend students' understanding of new vocabulary. Student activities include, for example, writing a script and recording an audio podcast that highlights important aspects of words, building a semantic web using Popplet (https://popplet.com), or developing a digital word wall with Padlet. Additionally, students can use ThingLink and PowerPoint to illustrate their words and add audio to create an online dictionary of sorts. By using various apps and digital tools, students expand on word learning electronically, rather than using pencil and paper. According to Dana Grisham, Linda Smetana, and Thomas Devere Wolsey (2015), reports from student teachers indicate that students at the upper elementary and secondary levels learn content-area vocabulary more deeply by connecting images, classroom discussion, writing, and technology to extend their learning.

Word Talks

Word talks derive from a similar strategy called *book talks*, in which students give a brief (fewer than five minutes) presentation about a book they recommend to their peers for independent reading. Word talks are alike in that they require a student to give a brief presentation on one to three words that they feel are important for their peers to know. This strategy is, like some others in this chapter, excellent for general academic words rather than highly specific or domain-specific words.

Some teachers who use word talks schedule a certain day each week or month for students to give these presentations. Other teachers employ a rotation so that one student does a word talk per day, a few times a week. Because students teach their peers, it's important to make time for word talks because in our experience, students tend to find classmate-led discussion much more memorable than discussion led by teachers. Student-led discussion is rarer and often more memorable just for that reason, but students also often have a way of saying something in a different way than the teacher would say it that makes the information click with their peers.

What kinds of words should students share in word talks? Many students share from their independent reading as well as their media and technology use. Most teachers ask students to select words that they feel their classmates should know and to provide a rationale for choosing those particular words.

For example, in a high school word talk, one student selected the following words: *ascent*, *descent*, *decompression*, and *recompression*. Can you tell what the student was learning to do outside of school? Scuba diving. This student was studying and practicing to get her initial scuba certification and thought these words would be good to share because although they have scuba-specific meanings, they also apply to other situations.

Word talks are great opportunities for students to showcase their interests and expertise, but most important, they make clear that word learning is continual because they occur throughout the year.

Vocabulary Videos

Judging from the popularity of YouTube and the ease of making videos with most smartphones and tablets, there is no stopping the amount of interest in them, particularly among teenagers. Vocabulary videos (Dalton & Schmidt, 2015) draw upon that interest and tie it into word learning. The goal of vocabulary videos is straightforward—students demonstrate their understanding of specific words by creating fifteen- to forty-five-second-long skits. You should emphasize improvisation rather than following a script and encourage students to tell a quick story to help others understand the meaning of a word. Hold students responsible for learning all the words presented in the videos.

Bridget Dalton and Kimberly McDavid Schmidt (2015) suggest the following six steps.

1. Students select a word for their video. Teachers can provide a list of words from which students choose, or they can self-select. The words can be academic vocabulary from a specific content area or tier two words.

2. Students explore the meaning of the word. Using print or digital reference resources such as the Visual Dictionary Online (http://visual.merriam-webster .com) or Lexipedia (www.lexipedia.com), a visual thesaurus, students develop their understanding of the word. Students use these to create a large sign with their word on one side and the definition on the other. At the end of the video, students display the sign to connect the target word, the definition, and the skit in the video.

3. Students brainstorm how they want to illustrate the word in the video. They can also determine roles (scriptwriter, actor, videographer, and so on), but the overall goal is to help students remember the word through their brief skit.

4. Students record the skit several times. After filming, they review the clip to check for sound quality, facial and bodily expression, and impact. Primarily, they're trying to determine if the short skit will really help students understand and remember the word. Finally, they choose their best video to share with classmates.

5. Students present their video to the class. It is easiest to download all the videos to a file storage folder and project them from a laptop onto a large screen or whiteboard. Students provide feedback to their peers following each video, asking them to clarify word meaning if necessary.

6. Students publish their videos. How public to make the videos depends on student privacy issues; however, you can publish them on a classroom blog, YouTube (www.youtube.com), the school website, or a wiki.

Vocabulary videos require students to think deeply and demonstrate their understanding of words in a unique format. Teachers we've worked with report that students understand words at a more nuanced level than with traditional methods of learning words. The Learning Network (a part of the *New York Times*) sponsors a contest in which students create vocabulary videos using the same premise as this strategy—demonstrating word meaning through a recorded skit. In this case, students are limited to creating a fifteen-second video. Entries have included words such as *serendipity*, *turncoat*, and *bifurcate*. After watching a number of the videos, we think students not only were creative but clearly demonstrated their understanding of these words. You can view some of the engaging and informative videos in the online article "Words Gone Wild: The Student Winners of Our 15-Second Vocabulary Video Contest" (Schulten, 2013).

Recap

Secondary students are inundated with words from the moment they step into the school building in the early morning until the moment they leave. Classes are full of content-specific vocabulary; teachers present difficult terms to students at a rapid pace. Teachers must integrate current technologies and digital tools and applications into vocabulary instruction and independent learning and practice. As teachers, we need to respond with a mix of instructional strategies across the curriculum so that students get the message that words matter everywhere and that word learning is a lifelong necessity.

Digital Tools for Secondary Students

Evernote (https://evernote.com): Digital notebook for students to keep a personal vocabulary log or collect interesting words

Flashcard Stash (http://flashcardstash.com): Games and review

Free Rice (www.freerice.com): Games and review

Lexipedia (www.lexipedia.com): Visual thesaurus

Lingro (www.lingro.com): Dictionary to support native English speakers with complex online text and to support English learners with all online reading

LiveBinders (www.livebinders.com): Digital notebook

OneNote (www.onenote.com): Digital notebook for students to keep a personal vocabulary log or collect interesting words

Padlet (https://padlet.com): Digital word wall

Popplet (https://popplet.com): Concept map tool

ThingLink (www.thinglink.com): Images with key vocabulary for students to use as part of presentations and projects to show their understanding of important conceptual vocabulary

Twitter (https://twitter.com): Social media for students to demonstrate understanding of vocabulary by writing tweets

Visual Dictionary Online (http://visual.merriam-webster.com): Online dictionary including images to accompany words

NEXT STEPS

Consider the following questions individually or discuss them with colleagues or in literacy leadership team settings.

Teachers

- How do these strategies compare with vocabulary strategies you currently use? How are they similar or different?
- Select one strategy from each of the three categories that you or your teaching team can begin using within your content area. With your team, discuss why you have chosen the strategy and how you plan to implement the strategy.
- What digital tools do you currently use to integrate vocabulary learning?
- Preview a few digital tools and apps and plan how to use these within your content area.

Literacy Leadership Teams

- Review the three categories of strategies suitable for secondary vocabulary instruction. How would you have teaching staff engage with these strategies?
- How can you support teachers' implementation of these strategies?
- Do your teachers currently use digital tools and apps to support and extend word learning within their content areas? Why or why not?
- Preview several digital tools and share with teachers. Perhaps use them during a staff meeting or professional development session. Support teachers in integrating academic vocabulary and word-learning tools in specific subject areas.

CHAPTER 7

Vocabulary Strategies
for Special Populations

As we provide professional development in urban, suburban, and rural schools all over the United States and abroad, we see teachers expending great effort to meet the needs of the very diverse learners they spend time with each day. Students with severe reading and writing disabilities sit right next to multilingual students and others who are refugees from war and who have never even sat at a desk or held a pencil. In short, the spectrum of general education students is wide and varied, and the range of students with special needs seems to be growing.

In this chapter, we recommend ways to adapt vocabulary instruction so that it has the greatest impact on special education students and English learners (ELs). Keep in mind, though, that these recommendations are also excellent for *all* learners. Effective instruction connects with many types of learners, and by employing some suggestions made here, you provide multiple avenues by which your students can access and use the words you want them to use. These strategies work with all students, regardless of whether they carry any type of label about how they might learn differently or learn best.

Supporting English Learners

Students who are highly literate in a first language more easily acquire a second language (August & Shanahan, 2006). However, we cannot always assess how literate a student is in his or her first language, and we often cannot provide academic support in the first language. So it behooves us to support the learning of new English vocabulary through multiple methods—and the best methods we can find. Teaching English learners well includes so much more than using visuals. Rebecca Deffes Silverman (2007) notes that all of the following approaches are beneficial in teaching ELs vocabulary.

- Introducing words through the rich context of authentic children's literature
- Providing student-friendly definitions and explanations of target words
- Using questions and prompts to help students think critically about word meaning

- Giving examples of how to use words in multiple contexts, not just the way the text they are studying uses it
- Using visual aids to illustrate word meanings in contexts other than the literature that introduces the words
- Allowing students to act out the meanings of words when applicable
- Providing encouragement for students to pronounce the words
- Pointing out the spelling of the words (to connect to familiar spelling patterns, roots, and so on)
- Leading students in comparing and contrasting words
- Facilitating repetition of the words

Supporting Students With Disabilities

The vocabulary learning of students with learning disabilities has not been the subject of a large number of research studies, but there is an emerging consensus on what methods seem to best support these students (Sweeny & Mason, 2011). Independent word study (as in the list of twenty words for students to study on their own for a quiz on Friday) is not generally effective for learning-disabled students, and again, we have made the point in other parts of this book that this method is not ideal for students regardless of any label about their learning or their language acquisition. As Benjamin Munson, Beth A. Kurtz, and Jennifer Windsor (2005) note, methods that have been effective for students with learning disabilities are semantic feature analysis, semantic maps, and mnemonic devices with visual aids; rote memorization is ineffective compared with more interactive instruction and with the methods just noted. Additionally, some students with learning differences may need more exposure to unusual spelling or phonetic patterns than their peers in order to better understand new words.

Because the recommendations for both groups of students overlap, we believe that whatever makes instruction better for ELs and students with learning disabilities most likely also makes it better for general education students. However, at times, it's advantageous for a teacher to know specific strategies (or adaptations of strategies) to employ for these two special groups of students. In the following sections, we share a few of these strategies and provide some specific suggestions for activities to support them.

Making Instruction More Dramatic

One of the most important tweaks we can provide in our daily instruction is to add a bit of drama. There are different associations we make as educators when someone advises us to be more dramatic, so let us be clear here about our meaning. While we agree with the recommendations of Robert J. Marzano (as cited in Umphrey, 2008) to embed more instruction in story, we feel that adding drama to instruction goes further than this. To us, dramatic instruction begins with an enthusiastic and knowledgeable teacher. Upon that foundation, the teacher adds powerful anecdotes, poetry, or stories in addition to moving, speaking, and performing in ways that draw attention to the most important, discipline-specific words.

Dancing Definitions

The Dancing Definitions strategy allows the teacher to be as dramatic a performer as he or she wishes to be and also involves repetition by students. The repetition consists of students repeating the performance that the teacher has modeled to enhance the likelihood of remembering something about word meaning. Educator Augusta Mann (2016) invented Dancing Definitions. She has been a teacher and in-demand staff developer for decades. Her strategies are rooted in performance art. You can visit Augusta Mann's website (www.successfulteachers.com) to get acquainted with her work. Dancing Definitions is an excellent strategy to use before reading complex text; it gives students an initial walking around definition through rhythm, repetition, gesture, and context. We recommend the following five-step adapted process for using Dancing Definitions.

1. Preview the text you will use. Select words that are important to understanding the text, and consider the utility of the words outside the text. This is a wonderful opportunity to help students learn tier two words. Make sure you have a few critical words—certainly no more than ten.

2. Using all appropriate resources, such as online or print dictionaries, glossaries, and textbooks, create student-friendly, melodic definitions and what Mann calls *tag sentences*. These sentences closely match the definitions and use the words in a context that students can readily understand. For example:
    *   **Definition:** A summary is a shortened version—in your own words!—of something you read.
    *   **Tag sentence:** Read your textbook carefully in case the teacher asks you to write a summary.

3. At a minimum, include intonation and gestures in your definitions. You may also want to do so in the tag sentences. Continuing the example from number 2:
    *   A summary is a shortened version (make a shortening or cutting motion with both hands) in your own words (point a finger as if directly at a student or point at your mouth to indicate *your own words*) of something you read (use your hands to look like an open book). Read your textbook carefully (do the open-book gesture again) in case the teacher asks you to write a summary (make a gesture like a pen writing in the air).

4. Plan one or more short time segments during which you can teach the Dancing Definitions prior to reading the selected texts. You can watch Augusta Mann herself teaching a group of teachers the strategy on YouTube (Successful Teachers, 2011). This video will help you better understand the elements of rhythm and gesture. Visit **go.SolutionTree.com/literacy** for a live link to this resource.

5. Teach all the Dancing Definitions prior to studying the text. Revisit the Dancing Definitions and keep any anchor charts or word walls featuring them posted until you feel most students have mastered the words at a basic level.

Using Dancing Definitions in your classroom provides benefits beyond familiarizing students with academic vocabulary. The strategy can help them feel more competent and confident as they start reading complex texts because they already have a leg up on some of the vocabulary. The definitions you create (and they memorize) help students internalize structures and patterns that carry over to their own speaking and writing. And lastly, participating in Dancing Definitions is fun and collaborative. Some students will really shine as they chant and move, and some students will flounder a bit—and everyone will be smiling. Angela has yet to see students grumble, complain, put their heads down, start a fight, or ask to go to the restroom during a Dancing Definitions lesson.

Thirty-Second Vocabulary

The purpose of Thirty-Second Vocabulary (Moen, 2007) is to provide students with the opportunity to revisit and reinforce word meanings through the use of artifacts or a performance to convey the word's meaning. You can integrate this strategy into any content area and provide a nonlinguistic (and fun!) means of reviewing key terms and concepts. The four steps are as follows.

1. Students select a word from the unit list of words (or the teacher can assign words).
2. Students develop a pantomime or performance that represents the meaning of the target word.
3. Students individually act out or dramatize the targeted word. The duration of the entire performance should be between thirty seconds and three minutes. (Most performances are under one minute.)
4. At some point during the presentation, the student must pronounce the word correctly, provide the word's definition, and tell what part of speech it is.

As Marzano (2004) points out, this strategy brings a playful and fun atmosphere to building vocabulary. Thirty-Second Vocabulary serves as a fun, quick, and meaningful way to reinforce academic vocabulary.

Some good examples of this strategy exist on YouTube. A few of our favorites follow. (Note that they do not include step 4. You will have to remind students to add that.) Visit **go.SolutionTree.com/literacy** for live links to these resources.

- *Diversity* (Lantzman, 2014)
- *Haughty* (Perez, 2014)
- *Dirge*, *elegy*, and *requiem* (Pierce, 2014)
- *Novice* (Berlin, 2014)

Making Instruction More Visual

One way of supporting word learning in every language is through the use of as much visual support as possible. This is true not only for ELs and students with learning disabilities, but for all students. Robert J. Marzano, along with other noted education researchers, has commented extensively on this. It is especially important to remember, as Marzano notes:

> All the senses come into play in learning. In most classrooms . . .
> reading and lectures dominate instruction, engaging students
> through the linguistic mode. Learners also acquire and retain knowl-
> edge nonlinguistically, through visual imagery, kinesthetic or whole-
> body modes, auditory experiences, and so forth. Teachers who wish
> to take advantage of all modes of learning will encourage students to
> make nonlinguistic representations of their thinking. These can take
> many forms. When students make concept maps, idea webs, drama-
> tizations, and other types of nonlinguistic representation, they are
> actively creating a model of their thinking. (Marzano Research, n.d.)

Many of us who have taught for a long time know that often, sketching a quick image
on the board or locating an image online really helps when explaining a difficult concept
to students. Deliberately using visuals in many forms supports learners who struggle with
language (for whatever reason they might struggle).

A few easy ways to use more visuals in combination with vocabulary instruction include
the following.

Word Walls

Adding images to your word walls is one strategy for making instruction more visual.
Clip art figures or more realistic images are fine, and in some cases, student-created art
may be preferable. We have seen excellent word walls employing nonlinguistic support
in many schools, but one of the most memorable was a high school word wall devoted
to SAT words that included high-quality drawings by students.

Co-creating digital word walls using Padlet is another strategy for making instruction
more visual. Padlet provides the opportunity to link vocabulary words with images, links,
and videos that will support learners as they deepen their understanding of the words.
Use this tool during instruction with students, adding links and images in real time, or
embed the Padlet within your classroom website and have students add independently to
the shared word wall. You can find many videos on YouTube that show how teachers use
Padlet in their instruction, and we've included more information about the capabilities
of this tool in appendix A (page 107).

Illustrated Note Taking

Showing students how to take notes that include quickly drawn visuals can support
content-area learning. You can quickly transform many note-taking formats by adding a
visual or two, and we don't mean elaborately drawn figures. We mean quick line drawings,
stick figures, and symbolic representations. Digital tools can be helpful here. Students
could use LiveBinders or OneNote to record notes and add images from the web or use
the embedded tools within these apps to create their own symbolic representations. Digital
images also have the advantage of being easy to share with classmates or a small group.

Thinking Maps

Schools around the world have used visual tools called Thinking Maps (Hyerle & Alper, 2011) to help students visualize their thinking. Thinking Maps are a collection of visual tools to use for specific types of content or specific cognitive actions. They are easy to use with students of all ages and have decades of research support behind them. There are eight Thinking Maps that David Hyerle and Larry Alper (2011) identify.

1. Brace Map for analysis
2. Bridge Map for analogies
3. Bubble Map for description
4. Circle Map for conceptual understanding
5. Double Bubble Map for comparison
6. Flow Map for sequence
7. Multiflow Map for cause and effect
8. Tree Map for classification

Multi-Faceted Comprehensive Vocabulary Instruction Program

A more in-depth method of using visuals to support vocabulary instruction comes from the Multi-Faceted Comprehensive Vocabulary Instruction Program (MCVIP; Manyak, 2010). Research surrounding this program lasted three years and focused on the design and implementation of a comprehensive vocabulary instruction program in fourth- and fifth-grade classrooms of mixed English learners and native English speakers. Students in all three years of the project exceeded expected growth on a standardized test in general vocabulary knowledge and showed very large positive effect sizes on specifically taught words (Manyak, 2010).

Briefly, the protocol for teaching targeted words includes the following six steps.

1. Present a targeted word in the context in which it appears in text whenever possible.
2. Provide a student-friendly definition.
3. Provide multiple examples of the word's use.
4. Prompt the students to use the word or at least think about it.
5. Show and briefly discuss an image that helps students make connections with the word.
6. Conclude with a thought question or a quick interactive activity. A thought question would focus on an authentic application of the word in the students' experience. An interactive activity might be a quick, quiz-like formative assessment, conducted verbally or in writing.

This process works best with academic vocabulary (tier two words) that appear in informational or literary text that students must read. So, for example, if your class was studying the contributions and achievements of the civil rights leader Martin Luther King Jr., students might read about him being a charismatic leader. However, the word *charismatic* may be unfamiliar. Let's examine how you would use this word with the six-step process.

In steps 1 through 3, you would read and reread the part of the text that contained the word *charismatic* and call students' attention to it. Then you might say something like, "*Charismatic* is a word that means someone is charming or fascinating and he or she has the power to draw people toward him or her." Then you might follow with examples of charismatic people from pop culture, television, movies, music, and history—whatever might most resonate with the students at the moment.

Next, at step 4, you could ask the students to think about a charismatic person they admire. Partners could turn and talk with each other to share their ideas. Then, in step 5, you could type the word *charisma* in an online dictionary such as Shahi (http://blachan .com/shahi), which would provide numerous images and stock photos that demonstrate the characteristics of charisma. Or, you could show a quick video clip that conveys charisma in action.

Lastly, in step 6, you could provide a few scenarios and ask students whether they reflect someone being charismatic. Or you might show stock photos again, or use cartoons or clip art figures, and ask students to give a thumbs-up if they think each example shows someone charismatic or a thumbs-down if not. The negative images might be of a teacher teaching and students yawning or putting their heads down, a speaker at a podium speaking to a distracted audience, a singer singing and audience members frowning and holding their ears—you get the point. Note that the last step doesn't have to include additional visual images. It could instead include short example sentences presented verbally. You could ask, "Would you like to go to a movie starring a charismatic actor?" or specific, school-based questions like, "Was our principal charismatic at the assembly last week?" Multiple examples within multiple contexts are as important in the six-step process as the visuals.

If you run across words that you have not planned to use this six-step process with, you can also provide visual instruction that is quick, focused, and supportive of both vocabulary learning and improved literacy in general. You can quickly employ the word wheel, described in chapter 5 (page 59), when the need arises once you and your students have become comfortable with it. You can adapt the TIP chart in chapter 6 (page 76) for certain content and activities as a note-taking template or a task for small cooperative groups. These strategies were not part of the MCVIP research but can be highly effective.

You may want to develop a set of pictographs that match certain content. Students can use the pictographs in place of vocabulary terms, or sketch the pictograph alongside these terms, to enhance memory through the visual. For example, in a science unit on classification of animals, a certain symbol can always represent birds while another represents reptiles and yet another represents fish (see figure 7.1).

Figure 7.1: Pictographs.

In the study of literature, pictographs might include two stick people with a wall or line between them, symbolizing person-versus-person conflict, and an open book with a big question mark floating above it, representing theme. Other literary terms that could be represented in pictographs include *protagonist*, *antagonist*, *dialogue*, *point of view*, *author's purpose*, *foreshadowing*, and *flashback*. These terms can become more concrete and memorable with the addition of a well-done visual.

Lastly, don't forget, even on the fly, quickly sketching a visual on the board and describing it to your students may work wonders. With the advent and ease of using online image searches and videos, integrating visuals to support learning has gotten much easier. The more modes of expression we can tap into, the greater chance there is that a learner will understand the word differently than he or she did just moments before.

Making Instruction More Tactile and Kinesthetic

Methods that use concrete objects or body movements solidify memory because they require participants to convey information in ways other than simply linguistically; in doing so, they often make abstract information more tangible. Learning simply feels different when students touch things and move about as part of the learning.

Modeling nonverbal communication is effective, as we mentioned earlier, but there is also evidence that asking students to express their understanding nonverbally increases their learning. Eric Jensen (2010) accurately sums up what we know about students using gestures:

> Why do gestures work? One theory is that gesturing actually lightens cognitive load while a person is thinking of what to say. There is scientific support for this theory. . . . Another possible reason (my own theory) is that it makes the brain work harder to change the representation from an abstract idea to a concrete thought, hence, they learn better.

Most of us know someone who can hardly talk at all without using his or her hands. (Angela is one of these people.) Why does using one's hands when explaining something come so naturally? Because the gestures help support the words, or perhaps help the person arrive at or solidify new ideas. The hands and the brain work together.

One of the most convincing studies about gestures in instruction focuses on mathematics learning in elementary school (Sime, 2006). This study found that adding gestures to spoken instructions makes those instructions more effective. Students given instruction that included a correct problem-solving strategy using gestures were significantly more likely to produce that strategy in their own gestures during the same instruction period than students not exposed to the gesture. The students in the experimental group were then far more likely to succeed on a post-test than students who did not produce the strategy in gesture. In summary, a teacher's gesture during instruction encourages students to produce gestures of their own, which, in turn, leads to deeper learning—or, as the researchers say, "Children may be able to use their hands to change their minds" (Sime, 2006, p. 211).

As we explained in the section on making instruction more dramatic, when a teacher uses gestures, intonation, rhythm, and other performance techniques, students often pay better attention. When teachers encourage students to use gestures, rhythm, and repetition, they tap into various learning pathways and therefore are more likely to remember the content that those actions convey. Building from this concept, we consider ways students may be involved with academic vocabulary while using their hands and bodies to make deeper connections to the words.

Using Objects

At times, giving students concrete objects to work with can enhance their learning like nothing else. For example, many elementary mathematics teachers know that base ten blocks are almost unparalleled as an aid to teaching place value. Consider objects that you can use to teach conceptual vocabulary, such as the following.

- Balls of various sizes to represent the sun and the planets with string to show the orbits of all the bodies. The sizes of the balls are correlated and in scale with the actual sizes of the planets.
- Paper cutouts or tongue depressor sticks drawn to represent characters and important parts of the setting in a short story or novel (students can use these cutouts when discussing the book). These can help students understand character traits and other literary elements better.
- Pipe cleaners or modeling clay that students can form into shapes to represent content. This helps students think symbolically and more deeply internalize the content.
- Paper clips, rubber bands, and other common objects found in schools—be creative and think about shapes they can take. Again, when students create models, they can more deeply internalize the content represented by the models.

Using the Tableau Strategy

Tableau is a reading comprehension strategy popularized by Jeffrey Wilhelm (2002). The name of this strategy comes from the French *tableau vivant*, which translates to a "living picture." In other words, actors present a scene but remain silent and motionless as if frozen in a photo. Students must create a freeze frame, without talking to the audience, to communicate the meaning of a concept. Obviously, students must truly understand the meaning of the idea they are presenting in order to communicate it using this kind of physicality.

You can use this strategy with literature very easily. Imagine, for instance, asking students (in small groups) to create a tableau that demonstrates how the Capulets and Montagues feel about each other in Act I of *Romeo and Juliet* (Shakespeare, n.d.), and then bring the strategy out again at the end of the play. Or ask students, again in small groups, to create a tableau to show what they think happened after the unclear ending of the classic short story "The Lady, or the Tiger?" (Stockton, 1882). Then let other students guess from observing each tableau as to the position of the group—did the character live with the beautiful maiden, or was he mauled by the beast?

Some teachers use the tableau strategy with informational text rather than literary, or with other material they need to cover in class. A good general explanation of the tableau strategy is available on YouTube (ArtsEducationOnline, 2009). This video is based on the book *A Dramatic Approach to Reading Comprehension: Strategies and Activities for Classroom Teachers* by Lenore Blank Kelner and Rosalind Flynn (2006). Visit **go.SolutionTree.com /literacy** for a live link to this video.

We encourage you to think about the support you already provide for your EL students and students with disabilities (and other students who struggle with language). In our experience, kinesthetic strategies are perhaps the least used, yet effective, type of strategy that teachers have at their disposal. We concur with Susan Griss (2013) when she says:

> For the sake of awakening and engaging our students in today's stressful, high-stakes academic climate, teachers can find new inspiration by embracing kinesthetic teaching. They need not be dancers or even comfortable with their bodies in order to use kinesthetic techniques effectively; they need only learn how to recognize the links between curriculum and creative movement, and then ask their students to embody learning.

Using Movement

Allowing students to move and use their bodies to represent ideas is a great way to deepen vocabulary knowledge. An added benefit is that students need as much physical activity as we can fit into our day, because we know many are probably too sedentary. Combining movement with content allows students to get up from their desks, which they love, and they connect motion with what you're trying to teach, which may enhance memory. Everybody wins!

Mathematics offers a wide range of topics that you can support through gestures and other movements. You can easily represent the following mathematical terms with gestures.

- *Greater than*, *less than*, and *equal to* (using extended arms)
- *Number line*, *coordinate plane*, and *plotting a point* (using people to represent points; the number line or coordinate plane can be made with tape on the floor or projected from a projector)
- *Area* and *perimeter* (using hand gestures that show an outline versus the whole)
- *Right*, *acute*, and *obtuse angles* (using extended arms)
- *Radius*, *diameter*, and *circumference* (having one arm extended, both arms extended, and arms in a circle)

In science, anything that consists of a series of steps or stages is a good candidate for students acting it out. For example, when students study open and closed electrical circuits in upper elementary or middle school, different actors can represent the switch, the person operating the switch, the current (moving to show how the current flows), the appliance, and so on. Food chains, the water cycle, the phases of the moon, the life cycle of a butterfly or frog, DNA replication—students can dramatize or physically represent all of these topics and many more.

In social studies and history, representing abstract concepts through facial expressions and gestures can help students remember a term in a visceral way and can also provide the audience with a visual memory to associate with the term. Some terms worth considering are *tyranny, democracy, anarchy, oppression, capitalism, imperialism, socialism, scarcity, dependence,* and *independence.* Terms that are more concrete are also possibilities. Students can certainly represent terms like *latitude* and *longitude* with arm motions or other movements they can create. They often confuse *emigrate* and *immigrate*; they can easily differentiate them with movements that show *out of* and *into.* Students could represent a bicameral legislature by pairing up and using a gesture or pose that shows both separation and togetherness. The list is endless if you put your mind to it and (perhaps) collaborate with other teachers.

In English language arts, one easy application is assigning the roles of narrator or speaker and the audience. Using students to represent an omniscient narrator, the characters, and the readers can make clear how an omniscient narrator operates versus a narrator with a more limited point of view. Students could represent the elements of plot in a short skit, pantomime, or tableau in which the climax clearly shows importance in comparison to the other elements. Character traits are also excellent for acting out—ask students to walk like a character in a certain scene or to show a facial expression in a critical moment of the story. Again, many possibilities exist. Let your brain roam around a bit, talk with colleagues, or do both—you will be amazed at what you come up with.

Creating Vocabulary Videos

Vocabulary videos (Dalton & Schmidt, 2015), which we described in full in the preceding chapter (page 89), merit another mention here. We can't understate the popularity and ease of creating videos. Using this strategy, students demonstrate their understanding of target words by creating fifteen- to forty-five-second-long skits that tell a brief story. Students can, of course, act these out within class, but the advantage to making short videos is that you can archive them on a classroom website for easy access and review.

Dalton and Schmidt (2015) recommend the following six steps. For a more complete version of the steps, see chapter 6 (page 89).

1. Students select a word for their video.
2. Students explore the meaning of the word using print or digital reference resources such as the Visual Dictionary Online (http://visual.merriam-webster.com) or Lexipedia (www.lexipedia.com), a visual thesaurus.
3. Students brainstorm how they want to illustrate the word in the video. They can also determine roles (scriptwriter, actor, videographer, and so on), but their overall goal is to remember the word through their brief skit. At the end of the

video, students display a sign to connect the target word, the definition, and the skit in the video.

4. Students record the skit several times and select their best video to share with classmates.

5. Students present their video to the class. (We suggest downloading the videos to a shared folder to make this easier.) Following each video, students answer any questions or provide further clarification about the meaning of the word.

6. Students publish their videos. We suggest publishing to a class website or YouTube, depending on your preferences and student permissions for visibility.

Displaying their understanding in this format, we believe, extends students' thinking and understanding of target words. You can view embedded videos of fifteen-second vocabulary skits in the online article "Words Gone Wild: The Student Winners of Our 15-Second Vocabulary Video Contest" (Schulten, 2013). Visit **go.SolutionTree.com /literacy** for a live link to this resource.

Building Oral Fluency and Competence

Often, teachers think of helping students become more effective oral communicators as being a specifically EL need. In our experience with diverse populations, many students need additional support and practice in presenting their ideas orally and in building up their academic vocabulary. We agree with Margarita Espino Calderón, Maria N. Trejo, and Hector Montenegro (2016) when they say that "the more limited the English of students, the more participation opportunities they should have" (p. 24).

All students with limited vocabulary need lots of practice speaking about academic content within a supportive culture. You may want to provide support for classroom discussion by providing sentence starters, sentence and paragraph templates, and plenty of modeling so that these learners actively participate in a rich variety of talking activities. Some useful sentence starters and sentence templates that we have found teachers use include the following.

- This sentence says that _____.
- One important fact, detail, or reason here is _____.
- To summarize, _____.
- _____ is similar to _____ because _____.
- _____ is different from _____ because _____.
- _____ is related to _____ in these ways: _____.
- I agree with _____ because _____.
- I disagree with _____ because _____.

Recap

English learners and students with learning disabilities need specialized support as they tackle complex vocabulary. Teachers should consider making instruction more dramatic, visual, tactile, and kinesthetic in addition to providing many opportunities for students to engage in classroom discourse.

Digital Tools for Special Populations

Free Rice (www.freerice.com): Games and review
Lexipedia (www.lexipedia.com): Visual thesaurus
LiveBinders (www.livebinders.com): Digital notebook
OneNote (www.onenote.com): Digital notebook
Padlet (https://padlet.com): Digital word wall
Popplet (https://popplet.com): Concept map tool
Shahi (http://blachan.com/shahi): Visual dictionary with multiple images and multiple definitions provided for each word
ThingLink (www.thinglink.com): Images with key vocabulary
Visual Dictionary Online (http://visual.merriam-webster.com): Online dictionary including images to accompany words

NEXT STEPS

Consider the following questions individually or discuss them with colleagues or in literacy leadership team settings.

Teachers

- Think about your current vocabulary instruction practices or those you've learned thus far in previous chapters. How do you currently differentiate instruction for ELs and students with learning disabilities?
- How do you see the instructional strategies for ELs and those with learning differences as similar to and different from those we discussed in previous chapters?
- Select a strategy to implement for a specific group of students. Perhaps commit to trying a strategy with a teaching partner. After trying, discuss successes or challenges with a colleague.
- Preview several digital tools and apps mentioned in this chapter. Select one or two to integrate into your instruction or review with English learners or students with disabilities. Which do you prefer or see students gravitate toward? Share with a colleague.

Literacy Leadership Teams

- What dramatic, visual, tactile, and kinesthetic strategies do you already employ? How could you share these on a larger scale?
- Which practices or strategies recommended in this chapter could make a real difference in the achievement of ELs and students with learning disabilities in your school?
- How can you best support teachers as they extend their repertoire of strategies for ELs and students with learning disabilities in your school or district?

Digital Tools That Support Vocabulary and Word Learning

In 21st century classrooms, digital tools often provide a richer and broader array of information about words and word meanings than do more traditional tools alone. And systematic, immersive, engaging word learning benefits students.

Digital tools have distinct advantages. Many tools allow teachers to easily customize words and word lists to support content goals so that students can practice, review, and play games with unit-specific words. For example, many tools allow students to do the following.

- Hear pronunciations
- Read words in a variety of authentic examples
- View photos and images related to words (especially important for English learners)
- Reinforce word learning through interactive games
- Play with and manipulate language
- Discover rhyming words
- Collaborate with classmates to create virtual word walls

The digital tools and games we discuss in the following sections show promise to support differentiated word learning, review, and language play. We group the tools into seven categories: (1) reference tools, (2) word clouds, (3) games and review, (4) concept maps, (5) word walls, (6) SAT and ACT preparation, and (7) classroom assessment. We include a summary and brief review of each tool; however, features frequently change, so be sure to check them out before using them with students. Several tools are particularly useful for supporting English learners, and we note these specifically. Like other digital tools and software, not all are created equal. Carefully choose tools that you can integrate into instructional routines that include practice, review, and deepening understanding of vocabulary (Tyson, 2013c). Visit **go.SolutionTree.com/literacy** for live links to these resources and to download the free reproducible "Using Digital Tools: Questions for Consideration."

Reference Tools

While traditional dictionaries can limit and sometimes downright confuse students, the variety of online tools holds promise for learning new words. Many tools include a visual display of words, vocabulary grouped by theme, and numerous examples of words used within context. The following list includes eleven online reference tools, many of which support English learners through visual displays. In addition to traditional dictionaries, we've also included several specialized dictionaries that support specific academic content. There are many reference tools from which to choose, depending on your content area, learning goal, and students' purpose and age level.

Lexipedia

When learning new words, students benefit from seeing relationships between the target word and other, perhaps more familiar words. Lexipedia (www.lexipedia.com), a visual thesaurus, is an excellent choice for an online, clickable word web. It's free and simple to use. Students type in any word, and Lexipedia instantly displays the target word along with additional words in a visual word web. Students can see complete definitions by hovering over each word. Lexipedia also color codes words by part of speech and relationship, such as noun, verb, adjective, synonym, antonym, and fuzzynym. *Fuzzynyms* are words that have a strong relationship to the target word; however, unlike with synonyms, replacing the target word with a fuzzynym would change the meaning of the sentence.

Lingro

Lingro (www.lingro.com) is another free, cool tool for both its wow factor and for its inherent usefulness. We think the *translate* and *learn* features are the two most useful. Simply type in a web address on the Lingro website, and the *translate* feature instantly turns the website into a clickable dictionary that translates text into Spanish, Chinese, Portuguese, Italian, or seven additional languages. Lingro adeptly hides in the background until students need it. To use it, students simply click on any word, and the definition of the word is instantly displayed in the language they choose. This feature is very useful for providing just-in-time support for English learners.

Lingro also includes a powerful *learn* feature that creates a word history list compiled from a student's history of defined words. Students can easily drag these words into word lists and create a title, such as "biology" or "*The Scarlet Letter*," for each. Further, the student can review the meaning of words in the lists by clicking on *games*, which turns the individual words into simple flashcards with definitions. Lingro is a powerful, integrated tool useful for English learners that makes complex text more accessible to all students.

A Maths Dictionary for Kids

In addition to traditional dictionaries, there are also specialized dictionaries based on topics, such as mathematics. This mathematics tool, available online for free, is advantageous for elementary through early secondary students and teachers. A Maths Dictionary for Kids (www.amathsdictionaryforkids.com) has our vote for usefulness, design, and functionality. It includes four features: (1) an interactive dictionary organized alphabetically that provides definitions, examples, activities, practice problems, and calculators; (2) a larger, quick-reference dictionary, which students can access from phones and tablets; (3) mathematics charts that include more than 280 well-designed, printable charts for teachers; and (4) a free app that includes one-page printable charts and guides for most mathematics topics from elementary through early high school.

Mathwords

If you're looking for a free, specialized mathematics dictionary for secondary students, Mathwords (www.mathwords.com) will likely meet your needs. Suitable for courses from beginning algebra to calculus, the site states it is "an interactive math dictionary with enough math words, math terms, math formulas, pictures, diagrams, tables, and examples to satisfy your inner math geek" (Mathwords, 2014). Terms are indexed in two ways—alphabetically and by subject area. For example, if a student desires to look up *probability*, it may be easier to search for the term from the alphabetical index. The entry for *probability* includes a definition, several formulas, and related words. For secondary mathematics students, the subject-area index is very useful. Students can search by topics including algebra, geometry, precalculus, and statistics, to name a few. While Mathwords is not a fancy tool, its subject-area usefulness deserves an A.

Shahi

For teachers searching for a free visual dictionary to support early learners, elementary students, and secondary students as well as English learners, Shahi (http://blachan.com /shahi) is a great choice. As stated on its site, Shahi is a visual dictionary that combines the resources of Wiktionary (www.wiktionary.org; a free online dictionary), Flickr (www .flickr.com; photographic images), and more. When a user enters a word, Shahi displays both a linguistic definition of the word as well as numerous visual images alongside the written definition. Within the definition, additional words are highlighted. If the user clicks on one of these words, additional visual images are displayed for the specific word. This is a new favorite for us because it's simple, straightforward, and a great nonlinguistic tool for students.

Snappy Words

Snappy Words (www.snappywords.com), another visual thesaurus, is similar to Lexipedia (www.lexipedia.com). Visually, the display is simpler, cleaner, and perhaps less distracting than Lexipedia, so it may work better for students who may be visually distracted. Since there are several online thesaurus tools, teachers may wish to introduce all of them and then allow time for students to explore and select a tool (or tools) that works best for them. Snappy Words requires an email sign-up for access to the site. Teachers of elementary students may wish to sign up to gain access for their students.

Visual Dictionary Online

Merriam-Webster's visual dictionary (http://visual.merriam-webster.com) is another online tool that is simple to use and available free of charge. In addition to the functionality to define single words, this dictionary features themes such as *astronomy* and *science* as well as more general-usage categories like *gardening* and *food and kitchen*. Clicking on these themes reveals more subcategories as well. Images often include labels that identify specific parts of the image, such as a plant cell, for example. Merriam-Webster's is very useful to English learners as they learn general tier one words that relate to the categories, such as *home*, *clothing*, and *transportation*, to name just a few.

WordHippo

An all-in-one free reference tool, WordHippo (www.wordhippo.com) is a straightforward resource that provides many different options related to learning words. It allows students to choose exactly the information they need, which may include the following: definitions, opposites, synonyms, antonyms, rhyming words, example sentences using words in context, past-tense words, and present-tense words. It also translates and pronounces words. The format of the site may appeal more to younger students, although the simplicity is suitable for all ages.

Wordnik

Wordnik (www.wordnik.com) is the world's largest online English dictionary, by number of words, according to the website. It includes several features that other tools do not. For example, there is a Word of the Day link that you can easily integrate into your morning meeting, bell-ringer activity, or end-of-day procedures. A Random Word feature provides an additional, unusual word that you can use any time you want to have some thoughtful discussion and promote curiosity about words. And, just for fun, the site tells you the Scrabble score for each Word of the Day and Random Word. Students (and teachers!) who enjoy Scrabble in its board-game form or its varied online adaptations may find that information useful.

Wordnik is unique in that it's also a social media tool. As part of the Wordnik community, students can read tweets with target words highlighted. They can also submit a phrase to be defined, a feature that's useful for English learners. When submitting a phrase, the user can see how other community members have used the designated phrase. We like the simplicity of Wordnik, and that it remains a free tool. Additional features include options such as *define*, *relate*, *list*, *discuss*, *see*, *hear*, and *love*. For example, if a user clicks on *relate*, Wordnik provides synonyms, antonymns, and the word within context. The user can hear a pronunciation of the target word by clicking on *hear*. By clicking on *love*, the user can add the word to his or her list of favorites. This reference tool is best suited to older students because the user needs to create an account and login password and because some of the featured words are intended for secondary students and adults.

Word Spy

Billed as the "word lover's guide to new words," Word Spy (www.wordspy.com) is the perfect dictionary to raise word consciousness among students. Word Spy, another free tool, includes a finite number of words, which are organized alphabetically, by tag or key word, and by date. The site also includes random words and, our favorite, the top 100 Word Spy words used within the previous seven days. Word Spy may be most suitable for secondary students or for those students who are fully invested in learning new words since it's more nuanced than traditional dictionaries. Word Spy also includes esoteric words and phrases that you may not see elsewhere, such as *Google dorking*, *food swamp*, *FOMO*, and *nerdsplaining*.

Your Dictionary

Your Dictionary (www.yourdictionary.com) describes itself as "clear, clean, uncluttered." And that's about right. While the home page is simple and distraction free, there are ads on the pages with definitions. Your Dictionary provides simple, straightforward definitions from several sources and claims to be the easiest-to-use online dictionary. Sometimes simple is good. In addition to providing definitions, Your Dictionary includes a thesaurus, places each word in context, allows students to create word lists and flashcards, and includes a reference feature. In addition, this free tool will save customized word lists when a user logs in with Facebook or Google. The Word Finder link allows users to enter the letters they may have been assigned in a game of Scrabble or Words With Friends and search for potential words to make. Your Dictionary also includes embedded social media tools allowing users to post words to Facebook, Twitter, and Google+.

Word Clouds

Word clouds, sometimes called *text clouds* or *tag clouds*, are a visual display of word frequency within a specific context, such as a speech, informational article, or blog post. Based on frequency data, words that appear more frequently appear bigger and bolder in the word cloud.

While word clouds arguably don't build vocabulary, they do develop word consciousness by allowing users to play with words, generate interest in words, and work with frequency data. You can also use word clouds to support instruction and curricular goals in a variety of ways. For example, when beginning a new unit in mathematics, students can brainstorm vocabulary associated with the topic. You can then easily display words in a word cloud, which would provide you and students with useful information related to words with which students have the most familiarity. In short, the tool can create valuable formative assessment information.

We present the following three tools that generate word clouds from least to most complex. Consider starting with the first tool before advancing to the others to see how you like it.

Tagxedo

Tagxedo (www.tagxedo.com), a free word cloud tool, bills itself as a word cloud with style, and we have to agree. It provides a good deal of customization for users. For example, Tagxedo is the right tool for the job if teachers or students want to create word clouds in specific shapes, such as an apple, tree, or mathematics symbol (see figure A.1). For younger students, Wordle (discussed in the next section) is much more straightforward to use; however, older students will love the customization Tagxedo provides, which includes colors, shapes, fonts, and themes. An important caveat to remember is that students need to use the tool for exploration of words and not get too caught up in the design itself.

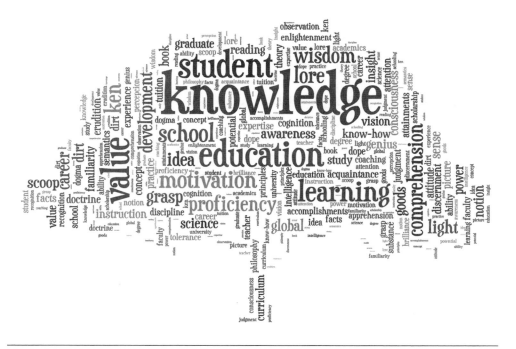

Figure A.1: Tagxedo example.

Wordle

Wordle (www.wordle.net), a free word cloud tool, generates word clouds based on any text entered (see figure A.2). Students can type in their own text or copy and paste a chunk of text from another source, and Wordle generates a word cloud of the key vocabulary. This tool allows students to select different fonts, layouts, and color schemes. They can print the word cloud or save it to their desktop.

You can use Wordles to support many educational and standards-based purposes, such as using them in a bell-ringer activity, to support note taking or other types of writing, or for reviewing content. See Dunn (2010) for a compilation of forty-five interesting ideas for integrating Wordle.

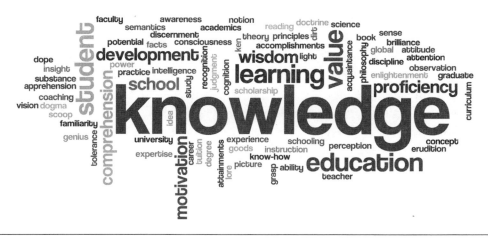

Figure A.2: Wordle example.

WordSift

Similar to with Wordle, you can type (or copy and paste) a piece of text into WordSift (http://wordsift.com), and it sorts the text based on word frequency (see figure A.3). Though not shown in figure A.3, additional WordSift features include noting the most frequently used word and the sentences in which the word is used. This free tool can also display a visual thesaurus beneath the word cloud. With the visual thesaurus, students immediately see how words are grouped semantically. This feature proves to be a useful addition to help students think more deeply and make connections between and among words.

Figure A.3: WordSift example.

Games and Review

As we mentioned previously, providing multiple opportunities for students to engage with words is an essential component of word learning. Playing games and providing opportunities to review words is an important part of a systematic approach to building vocabulary. Additionally, the game-like aspect, which can involve earning points and rewards, can motivate some students. Research by Sandra Schamroth Abrams and Sara Walsh (2014) involving eleventh-grade students using online digital tools to review vocabulary shows positive results for incorporating game-like activities into instruction. Abrams and Walsh (2014) report that individualized feedback helps students acquire vocabulary independently and that digital tools support vocabulary instruction. Students in the experimental group appeared to be more motivated, self-directed learners who enjoyed receiving immediate feedback and points awarded through an online vocabulary tool.

English Vocabulary Word Lists

English Vocabulary Word Lists (www.manythings.org/vocabulary) includes numerous handy word lists accompanied by games, quizzes, and puzzles. Originally designed for English learners, it benefits native English speakers as well. A link at the top of the home page takes students directly to resources designed for use with the iPad, including read-alouds and games that are customized so they can be played on small devices.

Flashcard Stash

While some consider flashcards an ineffective instructional method, students can benefit from instantly recognizing words or being fluent, if you will, with a specific set of words. Keep in mind, if understanding doesn't go deeper than instant recognition, students are probably in trouble—but instant recognition can be an important stepping stone to deeper understanding. Flashcard Stash (http://flashcardstash.com) allows teachers to sign up for a free account and create flashcards to coordinate with units of study. Students can also look up any word and save it to a flashcard. In addition, students can read target words in context, view synonyms, and hear each word pronounced.

Free Rice

Free Rice (www.freerice.com), an online game-like activity, is a personal favorite of ours. Students (and teachers) can practice matching words to the correct definitions and donate rice at the same time. For each correct answer, the United Nations World Food Programme donates ten grains of rice to a country in need. How's that for combining word learning with social consciousness? As users play, they see a visual display of rice added to a bowl each time they make a correct response. Free Rice includes subject-area lists in geography, science, mathematics, and others. With sixty levels, students can differentiate their play so they can have just the right level of challenge for them. In order to provide this customized experience, each student must have a login and password. One cautionary note: Free Rice may be addicting for your students *and* you.

VocabAhead

VocabAhead (www.vocabahead.com), available both as an online tool and as a mobile app, is a useful, nonlinguistic tool for students. Access is available by registering with an email address. Short videos (averaging thirty to sixty seconds) accompany each word, which makes VocabAhead a standout tool for secondary students. This tool features the Study Room, for students in grades 6–12, which includes leveled word lists and those geared toward ACT and SAT preparation. Students can view videos, hear pronunciations, practice, take quizzes, play games, track their performance, and more. For elementary students, teachers can create custom word lists and share them with students by embedding them in a blog or class website, which makes integration and review a snap.

Vocabulary Games

Vocabulary Games (www.vocabulary.co.il) provides free access to an array of vocabulary games that you could easily use on an interactive whiteboard for review purposes. Games vary widely and include those geared for the specific review of the following topics: compound words, prefixes and root words, test preparation, synonyms and antonyms, wordplay games, and many more. Some games appeal to elementary students, with names like Higgy Piggy, and others, such as SAT Word-o-Rama, are more suitable for high school students. This site provides a wealth of games from which to choose, and you can use them for review or even as a reward for the whole class or individuals.

VocabularySpellingCity

VocabularySpellingCity (www.spellingcity.com) includes many game-like activities useful for reviewing words. The site features a number of teacher-made lists including analogies, compound words, and mathematics words. The Teach Me feature pronounces words and uses each word in context. You can use preselected sentences or create your own. The free version allows you to save word lists and incorporate spelling quizzes. VocabularySpellingCity is a useful tool for students, teachers, and parents. While there are both a free and paid version, the paid version allows you to track student data, provide differentiated instruction, and access many more games for students. We think the paid subscription to VocabularySpellingCity could be a worthwhile resource for parent-teacher organizations or a business partnering with a school to fund.

Concept Maps

Concept maps help students see the logical or causal relationships among topics, events, or issues. For example, the defining or overarching topic typically appears in a large circle or box with subtopics in smaller circles or boxes surrounding the topic. Lines connect the shapes, which help visually define the relationships. When students develop concept maps themselves, they tap into higher-order-thinking skills by determining and defining interrelationships among ideas, topics, or concepts. By engaging in rich discussions about the topic and relationships between and among ideas or concepts, students have the opportunity to build and expand their vocabulary and word knowledge.

Popplet

Popplet (https://popplet.com) is a free, web-based digital tool and app that allows students to create their own concept maps. Using this concept-mapping app, students can independently or collaboratively develop and represent connections among ideas, topics, or concepts. As a collaborative tool, it works well for both creating and sharing maps with other groups of students. Students can ask and respond to questions about the relationships within maps. While students can develop maps using the more traditional pencil-and-paper method, Popplet has the distinct advantage of allowing them to easily revise their thinking and alter their maps based on additional research and feedback from peers. Students can also customize their maps, adding color, images, and videos. Finally, they can easily export their maps as images or PDFs (see figure A.4).

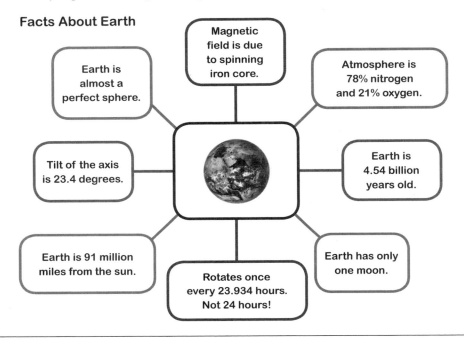

Figure A.4: Popplet concept map example.

Bubbl.us

Bubbl.us (https://bubbl.us) is another web-based app that can be used to create concept maps. The format is simple to use and easily creates a visual concept map sometimes referred to as a *mind map*. The free version only allows the user to create three mind maps in a month, which limits its usefulness with a class. There are also paid versions that provide for unlimited mind maps along with additional features.

MindMap

MindMap (http://goo.gl/XIkPfo) is a free Google Chrome extension that users can add to their browser. While this tool is similar to other free tools mentioned previously, an advantage of MindMap is that it is supported by tools such as Google Drive and Dropbox so users can work on mind maps anywhere and easily share them with others. MindMap also allows users to easily add images, URLs, and videos, which can be helpful when learning about concepts.

Word Walls

Interactive word walls can be the perfect tool to accompany an academic unit of study. As a space where students and teachers can routinely add words or as a dynamic part of a lesson, online word walls are a great addition to the more traditional word wall. In this section, we describe tools that you can use as dynamic, collaborative word walls accessible from any mobile device.

ThingLink

ThingLink (www.thinglink.com) is an online tool for making images dynamic and interactive. Simply upload an image, identify hotspots on specific parts of the image, and add text or web links. In the classroom, you can use ThingLink to launch a unit of study by introducing students to key vocabulary linked to an image. Students, on the other hand, could design interactive images as a means to achieve mastery in specific units. ThingLink is available in both free and paid versions. Browse the ThingLink site to see how dynamic the images become and how your students could benefit by developing and using them to learn new academic vocabulary.

Padlet

Padlet (https://padlet.com), formerly known as Wallwisher, is an online space to create a collaborative, digital word wall. Getting a leg up on the more traditional word wall, Padlet allows users to create sticky notes that can include text, images, links, and videos. You can embed these creations in a classroom website or blog, which makes it a go-to collaborative space for students. You can also use them during class discussion so that students can see their responses posted in real time. For primary students, teachers will probably want to create the wall ahead of time with words and links for students. Older students get the hang of the tool fairly quickly and can use it independently. Padlet is an easy-to-use, collaborative tool and can serve as a virtual classroom space to build online references and key vocabulary for content units. Padlet has both free and paid versions with varied capabilities. Learn more about how to integrate Padlet into your classroom by viewing the YouTube video *How to Use Padlet* (Byrne, 2013). Visit **go.SolutionTree .com/literacy** for a live link to this resource.

SAT and ACT Preparation

For students preparing for the SAT and ACT, the following four tools are very useful. While building vocabulary may be the primary goal of each tool, strengthening broad and specific vocabulary helps secondary students tackle the test comprehension passages more effectively and raise their scores. Kimberly's son, who is at this stage in his academic career, uses these apps daily to review vocabulary while riding the bus to and from school. Apps sure take up much less room than the stacks of cards from earlier generations!

PrepFactory

PrepFactory (www.prepfactory.com) is a free, web-based tool that serves as a great resource for ACT or SAT preparation. A comprehensive tool, PrepFactory includes videos ranging from an overview of the ACT and SAT to those that cover each academic area. It also includes videos that support specific preparation in reading, English, writing, mathematics, and science, as well as practice questions. Additional resources include ACT and SAT tips and tricks for each area and two game-like reviews called Wordplay and Numberplay.

Wordplay, the vocabulary tool, gives students a fun and interactive way of reviewing words in a competitive game that pits them against friends or randomly assigned online students to earn points based on accuracy and response speed. There is even a leaderboard that highlights top players of the day for competitive students. A chart tracks how many wins students have had in Wordplay and the level at which they're practicing. In addition to all the student tools, teachers can upload class rosters and track student progress. We both give PrepFactory two thumbs up for comprehensiveness, usefulness, and adding fun and competition to vocabulary review! (This tool is another that we should warn you about for its addictive tendencies.)

SAT Vocab by Brainscape

SAT Vocab by Brainscape is the most powerful of the four SAT prep tools we have included here and also bears the most expensive price tag. However, compared to expensive SAT prep courses, it's cheap. It offers both iOS and Android versions. SAT Vocab not only contains an extensive number of words (more than 1,400), it also includes more than three hundred word elements, such as prefixes, suffixes, and root words. As students move through words, they can rate how well they know each word when responding—that is, whether they guessed or were very confident in their response. The app repeats words intermittently based on a user's rating.

SAT Vocab by MindSnacks

For game-based review, SAT Vocab by MindSnacks may be the best choice. This free app is available on iTunes and provides fun, varied games to practice and review words. Levels allow students to advance as they become more proficient. Some games primarily involve instant recognition, while others are context based and require the student to determine which word fits best in the sentence. A limited selection of games is free; however, to access all the games, the user must upgrade and pay a small fee.

Vocabador

Vocabador, an inexpensive iPhone app, does everything you want digital flashcards to do, but within the engaging context of wrestling matches. The app levels its approximately four hundred words by difficulty so students can challenge themselves as they become more proficient. In addition, students can hear an audio pronunciation of the word; see synonyms, antonyms, and the part of speech; and read the word in context. Quiz games provide a fun way to review words, and this one may be especially appealing because of the fun wrestling theme.

Classroom Assessment

Teachers can easily use digital tools and apps for formative assessment purposes. They can use them to check for general word knowledge as well as for specific academic vocabulary within content areas. Apps range from simple quizzing tools to those that are well suited for supporting an engaging, game-like format in the classroom.

Kahoot!

Kahoot! (https://getkahoot.com) is a site that allows teachers to create multiple-choice items and turn them into games in which students use their devices to select answers before time runs out. Data on the results are instantly displayed. Teachers who use Kahoot! can also share the tasks they created on the tool's website. There are more than ten million public Kahoot! quizzes already housed there. Search terms like *literary devices* and *mathematics vocabulary* that focus on vocabulary yield dozens of Kahoot! games that teachers have shared.

Plickers

Plickers (www.plickers.com) are cards containing QR codes that teachers create and print. Students hold up the cards in response to questions posed to the whole class. The way students turn their cards reflects each student's answer choice (usually A, B, C, or D for multiple-choice items). The teacher simply snaps a photo of the entire class holding up their individual cards, using a phone or tablet. Then the Plickers app reads all the cards and shows the teacher real-time data about the students' answers. No devices are required for students to participate; they need only to hold up their preprinted cards with the QR code displayed.

Socrative

Socrative (www.socrative.com) is a tool that allows you to ask preplanned questions or questions in the moment and instantly compile data about how well students did. Students can access Socrative using desktop computers, laptops, tablets, or phones.

Twitter

Although it's best known as a social media platform, Twitter (https://twitter.com) can be successfully used as a quick formative assessment tool for vocabulary in classrooms where students have access to it. For example, students can be asked to compose and post a tweet using a recently learned vocabulary word. Twitter can also be used for exit tickets. Students can respond to any question the teacher designs with a tweet before they leave class.

Suggested Books Containing Tier Two Vocabulary Words for Primary and Intermediate Grades

*Visit **go.SolutionTree.com/literacy** for a free reproducible version of this appendix.*

Following are some suggested texts you can use in your classroom to teach vocabulary. We have highlighted specific words contained within the texts that you can use as vocabulary words. The following texts and the highlighted tier two vocabulary words can be used with the anchored word learning strategy described in chapter 5 (page 66) or as targeted vocabulary words to highlight when reading a chapter book or novel.

Primary

Borden, L. (2005). *The journey that saved Curious George: The true wartime escape of Margret and H. A. Rey*. Boston: Houghton Mifflin.

- *neutral*
- *regulations*
- *essential*

Bottner, B., & Kruglik, G. (2004). *Wallace's lists*. New York: Katherine Tegen Books.

- *automatically*
- *dumbfounded*
- *torrents*

Brett, J. (1991). *Berlioz the bear*. New York: Putnam.

- *dedicate*
- *desperation*
- *lurched*

Bruchac, J. (2000). *Crazy Horse's vision*. **New York: Lee & Low Books.**

- *conquering*
- *defended*
- *trampled*

Bunting, E. (2006). *Pop's bridge*. **Orlando, FL: Harcourt.**

- *laborers*
- *scaffolding*
- *skim*

Campbell, N. I. (2008). *Shin-chi's canoe.* **Toronto: Groundwood Books.**

- *reservation*
- *residential*

Cannon, J. (2004). *Pinduli*. **Orlando, FL: Harcourt.**

- *atrocious*
- *exquisite*
- *ravenous*

Carrick, P. (2009). *Watch out for Wolfgang.* **Watertown, MA: Charlesbridge.**

- *dismantling*
- *seized*
- *wallowing*

Crimi, C. (2005). *Henry and the buccaneer bunnies*. **Cambridge, MA: Candlewick Press.**

- *abandoned*
- *reputation*
- *salvaged*

Cronin, D. (2000). *Click, clack, moo: Cows that type*. **New York: Simon & Schuster Books for Young Readers.**

- *furious*
- *impatient*
- *neutral*

Curtis, J. L., & Cornell, L. (2008). *Big words for little people*. **New York: Joanna Cotler Books.**

- *irate*
- *persevere*
- *privacy*

Diakité, P. (2006). *I lost my tooth in Africa.* **New York: Scholastic.**

- *benediction*
- *cluster*
- *compound*

Dotlich, R. K. (1998). *Lemonade sun: And other summer poems.* **Honesdale, PA: Wordsong.**

- *fragile*
- *glimmering*
- *lucid*

Emanuel, G. (2014). *The everlasting embrace.* **New York: Viking.**

- *fleeting*
- *fortunate*
- *reserved*

Fox, M. (2012). *Tell me about your day today.* **New York: Beach Lane Books.**

- *company*

Garland, S. (1993). *The lotus seed.* **San Diego, CA: Harcourt Brace Jovanovich.**

- *dormant*
- *scrambled*
- *unfurling*

Gravett, E. (2006). *Wolves.* **New York: Simon & Schuster Books for Young Readers.**

- *dense*
- *outskirts*
- *retreated*

Griffin, K., & Combs, K. (2001). *Cowboy Sam and those confounded secrets.* **New York: Clarion Books.**

- *confounded*
- *dejected*
- *peculiar*
- *conversation*
- *twitched*

Henkes, K. (1991). *Chrysanthemum.* **New York: Greenwillow Books.**

- *discontented*
- *dreadful*
- *fascinating*

Laminack, L. (2004). *Saturdays and teacakes.* **Atlanta, GA: Peachtree.**

- *glanced*
- *struggled*
- *trudged*

Levine, E. (2007). *Henry's freedom box.* **New York: Scholastic.**

- *arranged*
- *beckoned*
- *pried*

Martin, J. B. (1998). *Snowflake Bentley.* **Boston: Houghton Mifflin.**

- *authority*
- *grandeur*
- *infinite*

O'Connor, J. (2006). *Fancy Nancy.* **New York: HarperCollins.**

- *accessories*
- *escort*
- *stupendous*

O'Neill, A. (2002). *The recess queen.* **New York: Scholastic.**

- *gaped*
- *disaster*
- *record*

Ripkin, C., Jr. (2007). *The longest season: The story of the Orioles' 1988 losing streak.* **New York: Philomel Books.**

- *consecutive*
- *declared*
- *explosive*

Ross, R. (2005). *Arctic airlift.* **Buffalo, NY: Blue Fox Press.**

- *intent*
- *precise*
- *vast*

Sayre, A. P. (2007). *Vulture view.* **New York: Holt.**

- *fragrant*
- *preen*
- *vulture*

Schaefer, L. M. (2003). *Pick, pull, snap! Where once a flower bloomed*. New York: Greenwillow Books.

- *fragrant*
- *shrivel*
- *wilt*

Schotter, R. (2006). *The boy who loved words*. New York: Schwartz & Wade Books.

- *disburse*
- *percolated*
- *periphery*

Intermediate

Picture Books

Frasier, D. (2000). *Miss Alaineus: A vocabulary disaster*. San Diego, CA: Harcourt Brace.

- *devastated*
- *luminous*
- *miscellaneous*

Rappaport, D. (2001). *Martin's big words: The life of Dr. Martin Luther King, Jr.* New York: Hyperion Books for Children.

- *equal rights*
- *movement*
- *segregation*

Ryan, P. M. (2002). *When Marian sang: The true recital of Marian Anderson— The voice of a century*. New York: Scholastic.

- *magnificent*
- *momentous*
- *passionate*

Chapter Books

Applegate, K. (2012). *The one and only Ivan*. New York: Harper.

- the exit 8 big top mall and video arcade: *domain, beckons*
- the littlest big top on earth: *forage*
- imagination: *ponder*
- old news: *indifferent*
- children: *contemplating*
- Ruby's story: *mesmerized*

- hunger: *foraging*
- my place: *sullen*
- nine thousand eight hundred seventy-six days: *stunted*
- free Ruby: *luscious*
- the top of the hill: *savoring*

Creech, S. (1994). *Walk two moons*. New York: Harper Collins.

- *peculiarity*
- *suspend*
- *ornery*
- *miniature*
- *investigating*
- *assembling*

Creech, S. (2002). *Ruby Holler*. New York: Joanna Cotler Books.

- Chapter 2: *inevitably*
- Chapter 3: *inhabited*
- Chapter 5: *putrid*
- Chapter 8: *idyllic*
- Chapter 11: *contagious*
- Chapter 14: *maneuver*
- Chapter 24: *mortified*
- Chapter 28: *oblivious*
- Chapter 41: *foresight*

DiCamillo, K. (2013). *Flora and Ulysses: The illuminated adventures*. Somerville, MA: Candlewick Press.

- Chapter 1: *predicting, unassuming, contract, defiance*
- Chapter 2: *cogitation, profound*
- Chapter 3: *indomitable, tentative*
- Chapter 4: *cynic, illuminated*
- Chapter 5: *retreated, obliged*
- Chapter 9: *astonishing*
- Chapter 14: *preoccupied*
- Chapter 18: *treacherousness, cryptic, traumatic*
- Chapter 19: *inadvertent*
- Chapter 24: *malfeasance*
- Chapter 26: *relentless, ferocity*
- Chapter 33: *idiocy*
- Chapter 39: *inconsequential*
- Chapter 43: *treacle*
- Chapter 44: *treacherous*
- Chapter 45: *speculative*
- Chapter 52: *vanquished, banished*
- Chapter 65: *sepulchral*

Sachar, L. (1998). *Holes.* **New York: Farrar, Straus and Giroux.**

- Chapter 3: *stifling, perseverance*
- Chapter 4: *barren, desolate*
- Chapter 6: *despicable*
- Chapter 7: *defective*

Annotated Bibliography of Vocabulary Books to Integrate Into Word Learning

The following books and series feature vocabulary as the main ingredient! They can be used as read-alouds to spark interest and conversation around words and added to the classroom library for independent reading.

Banks, K. (2006). *Max's words*. **New York: Farrar, Straus and Giroux.**

Max, a wild-haired young boy, has a dilemma. Both of his brothers have collections—stamps and coins—and he has none. The only thing he loves is words. So he starts collecting them in unusual ways. Soon he sets off to collect words, cutting them out of books and magazines. His family thinks he is a little crazy, but Max has a purpose. He collects and sorts his words to write captivating stories.

Max's Words is a delightful story with illustrations that capture the look and feel of words from varied books, cereal boxes, and magazines. Kimberly particularly loves this story because she, too, has a word-loving daughter (now a young adult) who has been cutting words out of books, magazines, leaflets, and just about anything since she was able to hold scissors in her hands.

Cleary, B. P. (1999–2011). *Words are CATegorical* **series. Minneapolis, MN: Lerner Publishing Group.**

This series of books uses cartoon characters and humor to teach the critical attributes of words. These books make great read-alouds, and even fairly young students can also use them for independent reading because the goofy-looking characters and rhyming text support deeper understanding. This series covers not only parts of speech but other language arts topics like synonyms, homophones, and irregular plurals in an entertaining manner.

The titles in this series include the following, written between 1999 and 2011.

- *But and For, Yet and Nor: What Is a Conjunction?* (Cleary, 2010a)
- *Cool! Whoa! Ah and Oh! What Is an Interjection?* (Cleary, 2011a)
- *Dearly, Nearly, Insincerely: What Is an Adverb?* (Cleary, 2003)
- *Feet and Puppies, Thieves and Guppies: What Are Irregular Plurals?* (Cleary, 2011b)
- *Hairy, Scary, Ordinary: What Is an Adjective?* (Cleary, 2000)
- *How Much Can a Bare Bear Bear? What Are Homonyms and Homophones?* (Cleary, 2005a)
- *I and You and Don't Forget Who: What Is a Pronoun?* (Cleary, 2004)
- *I'm and Won't, They're and Don't: What's a Contraction?* (Cleary, 2010b)
- *Lazily, Crazily, Just a Bit Nasally: More About Adverbs* (Cleary, 2008a)
- *A Lime, a Mime, a Pool of Slime: More About Nouns* (Cleary, 2006a)
- *A Mink, a Fink, a Skating Rink: What Is a Noun?* (Cleary, 1999)
- *Pitch and Throw, Grasp and Know: What Is a Synonym?* (Cleary, 2005b)
- *Quirky, Jerky, Extra Perky: More About Adjectives* (Cleary, 2007a)
- *Skin Like Milk, Hair of Silk: What Are Similes and Metaphors?* (Cleary, 2009a)
- *Slide and Slurp, Scratch and Burp: More About Verbs* (Cleary, 2007b)
- *Stop and Go, Yes and No: What Is an Antonym?* (Cleary, 2006b)
- *Straight and Curvy, Meek and Nervy: More About Antonyms* (Cleary, 2009b)
- *Stroll and Walk, Babble and Talk: More About Synonyms* (Cleary, 2008b)
- *To Root, to Toot, to Parachute: What Is a Verb?* (Cleary, 2001)
- *Under, Over, by the Clover: What Is a Preposition?* (Cleary, 2002)

Curtis, J. L., & Cornell, L. (2008). *Big words for little people*. **New York: Joanna Cotler Books.**

Big Words for Little People sends the message that kids don't have to be afraid of using big words. As a read-aloud book for young children, the story features many words that have to do with kids' behavior that they may hear but not understand. The playful illustrations and story line help bring life to the meaning of each word.

Frasier, D. (2000). *Miss Alaineus: A vocabulary disaster*. **San Diego, CA: Harcourt Brace.**

When Sage misunderstands one of the weekly vocabulary words, *miscellaneous*, it quickly leads to total humiliation and a classroom disaster. *Miss Alaineus* takes a comical look at misunderstanding words. The author peppers the book with vocabulary words in context and provides definitions along the way. Not only is the story funny and delightful, but the illustrations are colorful and dynamic.

Miss Alaineus is a great read-aloud and one that can prompt much discussion and extension activities on words. In the book, the Vocabulary Parade is a yearly activity in which students dress up in costumes that depict their favorite vocabulary words. Schools across the country host annual Vocabulary Parades, and the author's website (www.debrafrasier.com) features many pictures of students in costume as their favorite vocabulary words; she also shares a collection of costumes on her Pinterest page (www .pinterest.com/debrafrasier/vocabulary-parade-author-debra-frasier). The author provides a free vocabulary kit for schools, including letters to send home to parents inviting them to attend the parade at their child's school.

Heller, R. (1987–1998). *World of language* **series. New York: Grosset & Dunlap.**

This series of children's books focuses on parts of speech and teaches important grammatical information in a stunning visual format. Heller makes even complicated topics like the indicative mood of verbs and demonstrative pronouns accessible and enjoyable. Because of some of the advanced terminology, these books are appropriate for older learners, who will recognize grammatical terminology in a context that makes sense and entertains them, while younger students will love the illustrations and rhythmic text.

There are eight titles in the series, and although all are worthy of consideration, at the very least, teachers should consider the books that focus on nouns and verbs. The titles are as follows.

1. *Behind the Mask: A Book About Prepositions* (Heller, 1995)
2. *A Cache of Jewels and Other Collective Nouns* (Heller, 1987)
3. *Fantastic! Wow! And Unreal! A Book About Interjections and Conjunctions* (Heller, 1998)
4. *Kites Sail High: A Book About Verbs* (Heller, 1988)
5. *Many Luscious Lollipops: A Book About Adjectives* (Heller, 1989)
6. *Merry-Go-Round: A Book About Nouns* (Heller, 1990)
7. *Mine, All Mine: A Book About Pronouns* (Heller, 1997)
8. *Up, Up, and Away: A Book About Adverbs* (Heller, 1991)

Levitt, P. M., Burger, D. A., & Guralnick, E. S. (2009). *The weighty word book.* **Albuquerque: University of New Mexico Press.**

This book and its sequel, *Weighty Words, Too*, consist of twenty-six stories, one for each letter of the alphabet. Each story appears in the form of a tall tale and ends with a pithy statement that highlights the specific vocabulary word that the story leads to. The authors present words as complex as *bifurcate, heresy, ostracize,* and *quixotic* in the context of the clever tales. The stories in both books are as delightful for adults to experience as they are for students to hear, and you can read a story aloud in only two or three minutes.

Newman, L. (2004). *The boy who cried fabulous.* **Berkeley, CA: Tricycle Press.**

Roger is a young boy who describes everything he is enchanted with along his walks as *fabulous*. His wandering causes him to be late to school every day. In order for Roger to get to school on time, his parents forbid him from using the word *fabulous*. Can he stop using the word *fabulous*? This charming story makes a delightful read-aloud for early learners and provides a great jumping-off point for a minilesson about synonyms.

Schotter, R. (2006). *The boy who loved words*. New York: Schwartz & Wade Books.

Many children love to collect small treasures—rocks, bugs, stamps, cards. Selig is a young boy who is a born collector of *words* and gathers them wherever he goes. This lovely illustrated picture book chronicles the journey of Selig as he *collects* and *disburses* words.

We love the way the author sprinkles tier two words throughout the story, and the clever way that the illustrator includes them within the beautiful illustrations. The back cover of the book also features a glossary of the seventy vocabulary words found within the story. You can use *The Boy Who Loved Words* in your classroom as a read-aloud. Along with introducing a delightful story, reading this book aloud provides context for each vocabulary word to discuss with your students.

Wimmer, S. (2012). *The word collector* (J. Brokenbrow, Trans.). Madrid: Cuento de Luz.

This book is as much a delight to those with an artist's eye as it is for those who love words. The beautifully illustrated book layers phrases and words across the pages as they tell the magical story of Luna, a young girl who passionately loves words. She not only loves words, she sprinkles them like magic to warm and comfort others. The wonderful read-aloud invites the reader to go along for the journey and perhaps think about the positive power that words can have on others. And, just maybe, your students will become collectors of words as well.

References and Resources

Abrams, S. S., & Walsh, S. (2014). Gamified vocabulary: Online resources and enriched language learning. *Journal of Adolescent and Adult Literacy, 58*(1), 49–58.

Allen, J. (1999). *Words, words, words: Teaching vocabulary in grades 4–12*. York, ME: Stenhouse.

Allen, J. (2007). *Inside words: Tools for teaching academic vocabulary, grades 4–12*. Portland, ME: Stenhouse.

Allen, J. (2014). *Tools for teaching academic vocabulary*. Portland, ME: Stenhouse.

Alvermann, D. E. (2008). Why bother theorizing adolescents' online literacies for classroom practice and research? *Journal of Adolescent and Adult Literacy, 52*(1), 8–19.

Applegate, K. (2012). *The one and only Ivan*. New York: Harper.

Aronson, E., & Patnoe, S. (1997). *The jigsaw classroom: Building cooperation in the classroom* (2nd ed.). New York: Longman.

ArtsEducationOnline. (2009, February 8). *A dramatic approach to reading comprehension: Tableau* [Video file]. Accessed at www.youtube.com/watch?v=Nlxw9qflKxk on May 9, 2016.

August, D., & Shanahan, T. (Eds.). (2006). *Developing literacy in second-language learners: Report of the National Literacy Panel on Language-Minority Children and Youth* [Executive summary]. Mahwah, NJ: Erlbaum.

Baer, J., Kutner, M., Sabatini, J., & White, S. (2009). *Basic reading skills and the literacy of America's least literate adults: Results from the 2003 National Assessment of Adult Literacy (NAAL) supplemental studies* (NCES 2009–481). Washington, DC: National Center for Education Statistics. Accessed at http://nces.ed.gov/pubs2009/2009481.pdf on October 18, 2016.

Banks, K. (2006). *Max's words*. New York: Farrar, Straus and Giroux.

Baumann, J. F., Edwards, E. C., Font, G., Tereshinski, C. A., Kame'enui, E. J., & Olejnik, S. F. (2002). Teaching morphemic and contextual analysis to fifth-grade students. *Reading Research Quarterly, 37*(2), 150–176.

Beck, I. L., & McKeown, M. G. (1985). Teaching vocabulary: Making the instruction fit the goal. *Educational Perspectives, 23*(1), 11–15.

Beck, I. L., McKeown, M. G., & Kucan, L. (2008). *Creating robust vocabulary: Frequently asked questions and extended examples.* New York: Guilford Press.

Beck, I. L., McKeown, M. G., & Kucan, L. (2013). *Bringing words to life: Robust vocabulary instruction* (2nd ed.). New York: Guilford Press.

Beers, K. (2003). *When kids can't read, what teachers can do: A guide for teachers 6–12.* Portsmouth, NH: Heinemann.

Berlin, M. (2014, November 6). *30 second vocab video novice* [Video file]. Accessed at www.youtube.com/watch?v=Vr_6FKrqvvg on May 10, 2016.

Biemiller, A. (2005). Size and sequence in vocabulary development: Implications for choosing words for primary grade vocabulary instruction. In E. H. Hiebert & M. L. Kamil (Eds.), *Teaching and learning vocabulary: Bringing research to practice* (pp. 223–242). Mahwah, NJ: Erlbaum.

Blachowicz, C. L. Z., & Fisher, P. (2004). Putting the "fun" back in fundamental. In J. F. Baumann & E. J. Kame'enui (Eds.), *Vocabulary instruction: Research to practice* (pp. 210–238). New York: Guilford Press.

Blachowicz, C. L. Z., & Fisher, P. (2006). *Teaching vocabulary in all classrooms* (3rd ed.). Columbus, OH: Merrill.

Blachowicz, C. L. Z., Fisher, P., Ogle, D., & Watts-Taffe, S. (2006). Vocabulary: Questions from the classroom. *Reading Research Quarterly, 41*(4), 524–539.

Bond, M. A., & Wasik, B. A. (2009). *Conversation Stations*: Promoting language development in young children. *Early Childhood Education Journal, 36*(6), 467–473.

Borden, L. (2005). *The journey that saved Curious George: The true wartime escape of Margret and H. A. Rey.* Boston: Houghton Mifflin.

Bottner, B., & Kruglik, G. (2004). *Wallace's lists.* New York: Katherine Tegen Books.

Brand, J., & Kinash, S. (2010). *Pad-agogy: A quasi-experimental and ethnographic pilot test of the iPad in a blended mobile learning environment.* Paper presented at the 27th annual conference of the Australian Society for Computers in Learning in Tertiary Education, Sydney, Australia. Accessed at https://works.bepress.com/jeff_brand/18 on April 28, 2016.

Brent @ EdTech.tv. (2015). *Todays Meet for classroom backchannels* [Video file]. Accessed at www.youtube.com/watch?v=s1Ip-V0F-70 on June 23, 2016.

Brett, J. (1991). *Berlioz the bear.* New York: Putnam.

Bruchac, J. (2000). *Crazy Horse's vision.* New York: Lee & Low Books.

Bunting, E. (2006). *Pop's bridge.* Orlando, FL: Harcourt.

Byrne, R. (2013, September 10). *How to use Padlet* [Video file]. Accessed at www.youtube.com/watch?v=UuzciL8qCYM on May 10, 2016.

Calderón, M. E., Trejo, M. N., & Montenegro, H. (2016). *Literacy strategies for English learners in core content secondary classrooms.* Bloomington, IN: Solution Tree Press.

Campbell, J. R., Voelkl, K. E., & Donahue, P. L. (1997). *NAEP 1996 trends in academic progress.* (NCES 97–985r). Washington, DC: National Center for Education Statistics.

Campbell, N. I. (2008). *Shin-chi's canoe*. Toronto: Groundwood Books.

Cannon, J. (2004). *Pinduli*. Orlando, FL: Harcourt.

Carleton, L., & Marzano, R. J. (2010). *Vocabulary games for the classroom*. Bloomington, IN: Marzano Research.

Carrick, P. (2009). *Watch out for Wolfgang*. Watertown, MA: Charlesbridge.

Casale, U. P. (1985). Motor imaging: A reading-vocabulary strategy. *Journal of Reading, 28*(7), 619–621.

Catts, H. W., Fey, M. E., Zhang, X., & Tomblin, J. B. (1999). Language basis of reading and reading disabilities: Evidence from a longitudinal investigation. *Scientific Studies of Reading, 3*(4), 331–361.

Cleary, B. P. (1999). *A mink, a fink, a skating rink: What is a noun?* Minneapolis, MN: Carolrhoda Books.

Cleary, B. P. (2000). *Hairy, scary, ordinary: What is an adjective?* Minneapolis, MN: Carolrhoda Books.

Cleary, B. P. (2001). *To root, to toot, to parachute: What is a verb?* Minneapolis, MN: Carolrhoda Books.

Cleary, B. P. (2002). *Under, over, by the clover: What is a preposition?* Minneapolis, MN: Carolrhoda Books.

Cleary, B. P. (2003). *Dearly, nearly, insincerely: What is an adverb?* Minneapolis, MN: Carolrhoda Books.

Cleary, B. P. (2004). *I and you and don't forget who: What is a pronoun?* Minneapolis, MN: Carolrhoda Books.

Cleary, B. P. (2005a). *How much can a bare bear bear? What are homonyms and homophones?* Minneapolis, MN: Millbrook Press.

Cleary, B. P. (2005b). *Pitch and throw, grasp and know: What is a synonym?* Minneapolis, MN: Carolrhoda Books.

Cleary, B. P. (2006a). *A lime, a mime, a pool of slime: More about nouns*. Minneapolis, MN: Millbrook Press.

Cleary, B. P. (2006b). *Stop and go, yes and no: What is an antonym?* Minneapolis, MN: Millbrook Press.

Cleary, B. P. (2007a). *Quirky, jerky, extra perky: More about adjectives*. Minneapolis, MN: Millbrook Press.

Cleary, B. P. (2007b). *Slide and slurp, scratch and burp: More about verbs*. Minneapolis, MN: Millbrook Press.

Cleary, B. P. (2008a). *Lazily, crazily, just a bit nasally: More about adverbs*. Minneapolis, MN: Millbrook Press.

Cleary, B. P. (2008b). *Stroll and walk, babble and talk: More about synonyms*. Minneapolis, MN: Millbrook Press.

Cleary, B. P. (2009a). *Skin like milk, hair of silk: What are similes and metaphors?* Minneapolis, MN: Millbrook Press.

Cleary, B. P. (2009b). *Straight and curvy, meek and nervy: More about antonyms.* Minneapolis, MN: Millbrook Press.

Cleary, B. P. (2010a). *But and for, yet and nor: What is a conjunction?* Minneapolis, MN: Millbrook Press.

Cleary, B. P. (2010b). *I'm and won't, they're and don't: What's a contraction?* Minneapolis, MN: Millbrook Press.

Cleary, B. P. (2011a). *Cool! Whoa! Ah! And oh! What is an interjection?* Minneapolis, MN: Millbrook Press.

Cleary, B. P. (2011b). *Feet and puppies, thieves and guppies: What are irregular plurals?* Minneapolis, MN: Millbrook Press.

Cobb, C., & Blachowicz, C. L. Z. (2014). *No more "look up the list" vocabulary instruction.* Portsmouth, NH: Heinemann.

Connor, C. M., Morrison, F. J., & Slominski, L. (2006). Preschool instruction and children's emergent literacy growth. *Journal of Educational Psychology, 98*(4), 665–689.

Cook, S. W., & Goldin-Meadow, S. (2006). The role of gesture in learning: Do children use their hands to change their minds? *Journal of Cognition and Development, 7*(2), 211–232.

Cooney, B. (1982). *Miss Rumphius.* New York: Viking Press.

Cox, D. A. (2014, August 23). *Microsoft OneNote tutorial* [Video file]. Accessed at www.youtube.com/watch?v=h07qZLLQc4I on May 9, 2016.

Creech, S. (1994). *Walk two moons.* New York: HarperCollins.

Creech, S. (2002). *Ruby Holler.* New York: Joanna Cotler Books.

Crimi, C. (2005). *Henry and the buccaneer bunnies.* Cambridge, MA: Candlewick Press.

Cronin, D. (2000). *Click, clack, moo: Cows that type.* New York: Simon & Schuster Books for Young Readers.

Cunningham, A. E., & Stanovich, K. E. (1997). Early reading acquisition and its relation to reading experience and ability 10 years later. *Developmental Psychology, 33*(6), 934–945.

Curtis, J. L., & Cornell, L. (2008). *Big words for little people.* New York: Joanna Cotler Books.

Dale, E. (1965). Vocabulary measurement: Techniques and major findings. *Elementary English, 42*(8), 895–901.

Dalton, B., & Grisham, D. L. (2011). eVoc strategies: 10 ways to use technology to build vocabulary. *The Reading Teacher, 64*(5), 306–317.

Dalton, B., & Schmidt, K. M. (2015). Bringing words to life through student-created vocabulary videos. In T. V. Rasinski, K. E. Pytash, & R. E. Ferdig (Eds.), *Using technology to enhance reading: Innovative approaches to literacy instruction* (pp. 73–79). Bloomington, IN: Solution Tree Press.

D'Anna, C. A., Zechmeister, E. B., & Hall, J. W. (1991). Toward a meaningful definition of vocabulary size. *Journal of Reading Behavior, 23*(1), 109–122.

Davis, F. B. (1944). Fundamental factors of comprehension in reading. *Psychometrika*, *9*(3), 185–197.

Davis, F. B. (1968). Research in comprehension in reading. *Reading Research Quarterly*, *3*(4), 499–545.

Diakité, P. (2006). *I lost my tooth in Africa*. New York: Scholastic.

DiCamillo, K. (2006). *The miraculous journey of Edward Tulane*. Cambridge, MA: Candlewick Press.

DiCamillo, K. (2013). *Flora and Ulysses: The illuminated adventures*. Somerville, MA: Candlewick Press.

Dolch, E. W. (1948). *Problems in reading*. Champaign, IL: Garrard Press.

Dotlich, R. K. (1998). *Lemonade sun: And other summer poems*. Honesdale, PA: Wordsong.

DuFour, R., & Eaker, R. (1998). *Professional Learning Communities at Work: Best practices for enhancing student achievement*. Bloomington, IN: Solution Tree Press.

Dunn, J. (2010, July 15). *45 interesting ways to use Wordle in the classroom* [Blog post]. Accessed at www.edudemic.com/45-interesting-ways-to-use-wordle-in-the-classroom on June 21, 2016.

Dunn, L. M., & Dunn, D. M. (2007). *Peabody picture vocabulary test* (4th ed.). Circle Pines, MN: American Guidance Service.

Emanuel, G. (2014). *The everlasting embrace*. New York: Viking.

Evernote Scott. (2012, April 12). *Evernote tips: The 11 amazing features that make using Evernote so freaking awesome* [Video file]. Accessed at www.youtube.com/watch?v=Ce2_gWZHBIs on May 9, 2016.

Fielding, L. G., Wilson, P. T., & Anderson, R. C. (1986). A new focus on free reading: The role of tradebooks in reading instruction. In T. E. Raphael (Ed.), *The contexts of school-based literacy* (pp. 149–160). New York: Random House.

Figurelli, S. (2015, May 26). *The Matthew effect* [Blog post]. Accessed at http://inservice.ascd.org/the-matthew-effect on January 23, 2016.

Fisher, D., & Frey, N. (2007). *Checking for understanding: Formative assessment techniques for your classroom*. Alexandria, VA: Association for Supervision and Curriculum Development.

Fox, M. (1989). *Wilfrid Gordon McDonald Partridge*. Brooklyn, NY: Kane/Miller Books.

Fox, M. (2012). *Tell me about your day today*. New York: Beach Lane Books.

Frasier, D. (2000). *Miss Alaineus: A vocabulary disaster*. San Diego, CA: Harcourt Brace.

Frayer, D. A., Fredrick, W. C., & Klausmeier, H. J. (1969). *A schema for testing the level of concept mastery: Report from the Project on Situational Variables and Efficiency of Concept Learning*. Madison: Wisconsin Research and Development Center for Cognitive Learning.

Fry, E. (2000). *1000 instant words: The most common words for teaching reading, writing and spelling*. Westminster, CA: Teacher Created Resources.

Ganea, P. A., Pickard, M. B., & DeLoache, J. S. (2008). Transfer between picture books and the real world by very young children. *Journal of Cognition and Development*, *9*(1), 46–66.

Garland, S. (1993). *The lotus seed.* San Diego, CA: Harcourt Brace Jovanovich.

Graves, M. F. (2000). A vocabulary program to complement and bolster a middle-grade comprehension program. In B. M. Taylor, M. F. Graves, & P. van den Broek (Eds.), *Reading for meaning: Fostering comprehension in the middle grades* (pp. 116–135). New York: Teachers College Press.

Graves, M. F. (2006). *The vocabulary book: Learning and instruction.* New York: Teachers College Press.

Graves, M. F. (2007). Vocabulary instruction in the middle grades. *Voices From the Middle, 15*(1), 13–19.

Graves, M. F., & Sales, G. C. (2013). *Teaching 50,000 words: Meeting and exceeding the Common Core State Standards for vocabulary.* Newark, DE: International Reading Association.

Gravett, E. (2006). *Wolves.* New York: Simon & Schuster Books for Young Readers.

Greenwood, S. (2004). Content matters: Building vocabulary and conceptual understanding in the subject areas. *Middle School Journal, 35*(3), 27–34.

Griffin, K., & Combs, K. (2001). *Cowboy Sam and those confounded secrets.* New York: Clarion Books.

Grigg, W. S., Daane, M. C., Jin, Y., & Campbell, J. R. (2003). *The nation's report card: Reading 2002* (NCES 2003-521). Washington, DC: National Center for Education Statistics. Accessed at https://nces.ed.gov/nationsreportcard/pdf/main2002/2003521.pdf on October 20, 2016.

Grisham, D. L., Smetana, L., & Wolsey, T. D. (2015). Post-reading vocabulary development through VSSPlus. In T. V. Rasinski, K. E. Pytash, & R. E. Ferdig (Eds.), *Using technology to enhance reading: Innovative approaches to literacy instruction* (pp. 65–71). Bloomington, IN: Solution Tree Press.

Griss, S. (2013, March 20). First person: The power of movement in teaching and learning. *Education Week Teacher.* Accessed at www.edweek.org/tm/articles/2013/03/19/fp_griss.html on January 23, 2016.

Haggard, M. R. (1986). The vocabulary self-collection strategy: Using student interest and world knowledge to enhance vocabulary growth. *Journal of Reading, 29*(7), 634–642.

Hart, B., & Risley, T. R. (1995). *Meaningful differences in the everyday experience of young American children.* Baltimore: Brookes.

Hart, B., & Risley, T. R. (2003). The early catastrophe: The 30 million word gap by age 3. *American Educator.* Accessed at www.aft.org//sites/default/files/periodicals/TheEarly Catastrophe.pdf on January 23, 2016.

Heller, R. (1987). *A cache of jewels and other collective nouns.* New York: Grosset & Dunlap.

Heller, R. (1988). *Kites sail high: A book about verbs.* New York: Grosset & Dunlap.

Heller, R. (1989). *Many luscious lollipops: A book about adjectives.* New York: Grosset & Dunlap.

Heller, R. (1990). *Merry-go-round: A book about nouns.* New York: Grosset & Dunlap.

Heller, R. (1991). *Up, up, and away: A book about adverbs*. New York: Grosset & Dunlap.

Heller, R. (1995). *Behind the mask: A book about prepositions*. New York: Grosset & Dunlap.

Heller, R. (1997). *Mine, all mine: A book about pronouns*. New York: Grosset & Dunlap.

Heller, R. (1998). *Fantastic! Wow! And unreal!: A book about interjections and conjunctions*. New York: Grosset & Dunlap.

Henkes, K. (1991). *Chrysanthemum*. New York: Greenwillow Books.

Herman, P. A., Anderson, R. C., Pearson, P. D., & Nagy, W. E. (1987). Incidental acquisition of word meaning from expositions with varied text features. *Reading Research Quarterly*, *22*(3), 263–284.

Hinchman, K. A., Alvermann, D. E., Boyd, F. B., Brozo, W. G., & Vacca, R. T. (2003/2004). Supporting older students' in- and out-of-school literacies. *Journal of Adolescent and Adult Literacy*, *47*(4), 304–310.

Hoyt, L. (2009). *Revisit, reflect, retell: Time-tested strategies for teaching reading comprehension* (Updated ed.). Portsmouth, NH: Heinemann.

Hutchison, A. C., & Colwell, J. (2014). The potential of digital technologies to support literacy instruction relevant to the Common Core State Standards. *Journal of Adolescent and Adult Literacy*, *58*(2), 147–156.

Hutchison, A. C., & Woodward, L. (2014). A planning cycle for integrating digital technology into literacy instruction. *The Reading Teacher*, *67*(6), 455–464.

Hyerle, D. N., & Alper, L. (Eds.). (2011). *Student successes with Thinking Maps: School-based research, results, and models for achievement using visual tools* (2nd ed.). Thousand Oaks, CA: Corwin Press.

International Literacy Association. (n.d.). *Standards for reading professionals—Revised 2010*. Accessed at www.literacyworldwide.org/get-resources/standards/standards-for-reading -professionals on January 23, 2016.

International Reading Association & the National Association for the Education of Young Children. (1998). *Learning to read and write: Developmentally appropriate practices for young children—A joint position statement of the International Reading Association and the National Association for the Education of Young Children*. Washington, DC: Authors. Accessed at www.naeyc.org/files/naeyc/file/positions/PSREAD98.PDF on January 24, 2016.

Jensen, E. (2010). *When clear instruction and visual aids are not enough* [Blog post]. Accessed at www.jensenlearning.com/news/when-clear-instruction-and-visual-aids-are-not-enough /brain-based-learning on January 23, 2016.

Jones, C. (Director), & Washam, B. (Director). (1966). *How the Grinch stole Christmas!* [Motion picture]. United States: CBS.

Kelner, L. B., & Flynn, R. M. (2006). *A dramatic approach to reading comprehension: Strategies and activities for classroom teachers*. Portsmouth, NH: Heinemann.

Laminack, L. (2004). *Saturdays and teacakes*. Atlanta, GA: Peachtree.

Lantzman, M. (2014, May 11). *Diversity (30 second vocab)* [Video file]. Accessed at www .youtube.com/watch?v=mA-E9s_zgZA on May 10, 2016.

LeRoy, M. (Producer), & Fleming, V. (Director). (1939). *The Wizard of Oz* [Motion picture]. United States: Metro-Goldwyn-Mayer.

Levine, E. (2007). *Henry's freedom box*. New York: Scholastic.

Levitt, P. M., Burger, D. A., & Guralnick, E. S. (2009). *The weighty word book*. Albuquerque: University of New Mexico Press.

Mann, A. (2016). *Secrets of successful urban teachers: Teaching strategies 1*. Accessed at www .successfulteachers.com/teaching-strategies-1.php on October 6, 2016.

Manyak, P. C. (2010). Vocabulary instruction for English learners: Lessons from MCVIP. *The Reading Teacher, 64*(2), 143–146.

Manyak, P. C., Von Gunten, H., Autenrieth, D., Gillis, C., Mastre-O'Farrell, J., Irvine-McDermott, E., et al. (2014). Four practical principles for enhancing vocabulary instruction. *The Reading Teacher, 68*(1), 13–23.

Martin, J. B. (1998). *Snowflake Bentley*. Boston: Houghton Mifflin.

Marzano, R. J. (2004). *Building background knowledge for academic achievement: Research on what works in schools*. Alexandria, VA: Association for Supervision and Curriculum Development.

Marzano, R. J. (2009). The art and science of teaching: Six steps to better vocabulary instruction. *Educational Leadership, 67*(1), 83–84.

Marzano, R. J., & Simms, J. A. (2013). *Vocabulary for the Common Core*. Bloomington, IN: Marzano Research.

Marzano Research. (n.d.). *5. Nonlinguistic representations*. Accessed at http://escmarzano .wikispaces.com/5.+Nonlinguistic+Representations on January 23, 2016.

Mathwords. (2014). *Mathwords: Terms and formulas from beginning algebra to calculus*. Accessed at www.mathwords.com on October 19, 2016.

McGill-Franzen, A., Allington, R. L., Yokoi, L., & Brooks, G. (1999). Putting books in the classroom seems necessary but not sufficient. *Journal of Educational Research, 93*(2), 67–74.

McKeown, M. G., Beck, I. L., Omanson, R. C., & Pople, M. T. (1985). Some effects of the nature and frequency of vocabulary instruction on the knowledge and use of words. *Reading Research Quarterly, 20*(5), 522–535.

Moats, L. C. (2001). Overcoming the language gap: Invest generously in teacher professional development. *American Educator, 25*(2), 5, 8–9.

Moen, C. B. (2007). Bringing words to life and into the lives of middle school students. *Voices From the Middle, 15*(1), 20–26.

Munson, B., Kurtz, B. A., & Windsor, J. (2005). The influence of vocabulary size, phonotactic probability, and wordlikeness on nonword repetitions of children with and without specific language impairment. *Journal of Speech, Language, and Hearing Research, 48*(5), 1033–1047.

Nagy, W. E., Anderson, R. C., & Herman, P. A. (1987). Learning word meanings from context during normal reading. *American Educational Research Journal, 24*(2), 237–270.

Nagy, W. E., Diakidoy, I.-A. N., & Anderson, R. C. (1993). The acquisition of morphology: Learning the contribution of suffixes to the meaning of derivatives. *Journal of Reading Behavior, 25*(2), 155–170.

Nagy, W. E., & Herman, P. A. (1987). Breadth and depth of vocabulary knowledge: Implications for acquisition and instruction. In M. G. McKeown & M. E. Curtis (Eds.), *The nature of vocabulary acquisition* (pp. 19–35). Hillsdale, NJ: Erlbaum.

Nagy, W. E., Herman, P. A., & Anderson, R. C. (1985). Learning words from context. *Reading Research Quarterly, 20*(2), 233–253.

Nagy, W. E., & Scott, J. A. (2000). Vocabulary processes. In M. L. Kamil, P. B. Mosenthal, P. D. Pearson, & R. Barr (Eds.), *Handbook of reading research* (Vol. III, pp. 269–284). Mahwah, NJ: Erlbaum.

National Governors Association Center for Best Practices & Council of Chief State School Officers. (n.d.). *Common Core State Standards for English language arts and literacy in history/social studies, science, and technical subjects: Appendix A—Research supporting key elements of the standards*. Washington, DC: Authors. Accessed at www.corestandards.org /assets/Appendix_A.pdf on October 18, 2016.

National Governors Association Center for Best Practices & Council of Chief State School Officers. (2010). *Common Core State Standards for English language arts and literacy in history/social studies, science, and technical subjects*. Washington, DC: Authors. Accessed at www.corestandards.org/ELA-Literacy on December 7, 2015.

National Reading Panel. (2000). *Teaching children to read: An evidence-based assessment of the scientific research literature on reading and its implications for reading instruction—Reports of the subgroups* (NIH Publication No. 00–4754). Bethesda, MD: National Institutes of Health. Accessed at www.nichd.nih.gov/publications/pubs/nrp/documents/report.pdf on May 11, 2016.

Newman, L. (2004). *The boy who cried fabulous*. Berkeley, CA: Tricycle Press.

O'Connor, J. (2006). *Fancy Nancy*. New York: HarperCollins.

O'Neill, A. (2002). *The recess queen*. New York: Scholastic.

Pacheco, M. B., & Goodwin, A. P. (2013). Putting two and two together: Middle school students' morphological problem-solving strategies for unknown words. *Journal of Adolescent and Adult Literacy, 56*(7), 541–553.

Perez, E. (2014, November 30). *30 second vocab video-haughty* [Video file]. Accessed at www .youtube.com/watch?v=I93wexL3jNg on May 10, 2016.

Pierce, H. (2014, October 31). *30 second vocabulary video* [Video file]. Accessed at www .youtube.com/watch?v=9IBuQQOymdQ on May 10, 2016.

Pondiscio, R. (2014). It pays to increase your word power. *Education Gadfly Weekly, 14*(50). Accessed at http://edexcellence.net/articles/it-pays-to-increase-your-word-power on January 23, 2016.

Pressley, M. (2002). Comprehension strategies instruction: A turn-of-the-century status report. In C. C. Block & M. Pressley (Eds.), *Comprehension instruction: Research-based best practices* (pp. 11–27). New York: Guilford Press.

Pressley, M., Disney, L., & Anderson, K. (2007). Landmark vocabulary instructional research and the vocabulary instructional research that makes sense now. In R. K. Wagner, A. E. Muse, & K. R. Tannenbaum (Eds.), *Vocabulary acquisition: Implications for reading comprehension* (pp. 205–232). New York: Guilford Press.

Rampell, C. (2013). College graduates fare well in jobs market, even through recession. *New York Times.* Accessed at www.nytimes.com/2013/05/04/business/college-graduates -fare-well-in-jobs-market-even-through-recession.html?_r=1 on October 18, 2016.

Rappaport, D. (2001). *Martin's big words: The life of Dr. Martin Luther King, Jr.* New York: Hyperion Books for Children.

Rice, M. L., & Watkins, R. V. (1996). "Show me X": New views of an old assessment technique. In K. N. Cole, P. S. Dale, & D. J. Thal (Eds.), *Assessment of communication and language* (pp. 183–206). Baltimore: Brookes.

Ripkin, C., Jr. (2007). *The longest season: The story of the Orioles' 1988 losing streak.* New York: Philomel Books.

Rollins, S. P. (2014). *Learning in the fast lane: 8 ways to put all students on the road to academic success.* Alexandria, VA: Association for Supervision and Curriculum Development.

Ross, R. (2005). *Arctic airlift.* Buffalo, NY: Blue Fox Press.

Roth, F. P., Speece, D. L., & Cooper, D. H. (2002). A longitudinal analysis of the connection between oral language and early reading. *Journal of Educational Research, 95*(5), 259–272.

Ryan, P. M. (2002). *When Marian sang: The true recital of Marian Anderson—The voice of a century.* New York: Scholastic.

Sachar, L. (1998). *Holes.* New York: Farrar, Straus and Giroux.

Sayre, A. P. (2007). *Vulture view.* New York: Holt.

Schaefer, L. M. (2003). *Pick, pull, snap!: Where once a flower bloomed.* New York: Greenwillow Books.

Schotter, R. (2006). *The boy who loved words.* New York: Schwartz & Wade Books.

Schulten, K. (2013, December 19). Words gone wild: The student winners of our 15-second vocabulary video contest [Video file]. *New York Times.* Accessed at http://learning .blogs.nytimes.com/2013/12/19/words-gone-wild-the-student-winners-of-our-15-second -vocabulary-video-contest/comment-page-1 on May 10, 2016.

Scott, J. A., Jamieson-Noel, D., & Asselin, M. (2003). Vocabulary instruction throughout the day in twenty-three Canadian upper-elementary classrooms. *Elementary School Journal, 103*(3), 269–286.

Scott, J. A., Miller, T. F., & Flinspach, S. L. (2012). Developing word consciousness: Lessons from highly diverse fourth-grade classrooms. In E. J. Kame'enui & J. F. Baumann (Eds.), *Vocabulary instruction: Research to practice* (2nd ed.; pp. 169–188). New York: Guilford Press.

Shakespeare, W. (n.d.). *Romeo and Juliet: A tragedy, in five acts.* London: G. H. Davidson.

Silverman, R. D. (2007). Vocabulary development of English-language and English-only learners in kindergarten. *Elementary School Journal, 107*(4), 365–383.

Sime, D. (2006). What do learners make of teachers' gestures in the language classroom? *International Review of Applied Linguistics in Language Teaching, 44*(2), 211–230.

Snell, E. K., Hindman, A. H., & Wasik, B. A. (2015). How can book reading close the word gap? Five key practices from research. *The Reading Teacher, 68*(7), 560–571.

Soliloquy. (n.d.). In *Merriam-Webster's online dictionary*. Accessed at www.merriam-webster .com/dictionary/soliloquy on June 6, 2016.

Spearritt, D. (1972). Identification of sub-skills of reading comprehension by maximum likelihood factor analysis. *Reading Research Quarterly, 8*(1), 92–111.

Sprenger, M. (2013). *Teaching the critical vocabulary of the Common Core: 55 words that make or break student understanding.* Alexandria, VA: Association for Supervision and Curriculum Development.

Stahl, S. A. (1999). *Vocabulary development.* Cambridge, MA: Brookline Books.

Stahl, S. A. (2004). Vocabulary learning and the child with learning disabilities. *Perspectives, 30*(1), 5–12.

Stahl, S. A. (2005). Four problems with teaching word meanings (and what to do to make vocabulary an integral part of instruction). In E. H. Hiebert & M. L. Kamil (Eds.), *Teaching and learning vocabulary: Bringing research to practice* (pp. 95–114). Mahwah, NJ: Erlbaum.

Stahl, S. A., & Fairbanks, M. M. (1986). The effects of vocabulary instruction: A model-based meta-analysis. *Review of Educational Research, 56*(1), 72–110.

Stanovich, K. E. (1986). Matthew effects in reading: Some consequences of individual differences in the acquisition of literacy. *Reading Research Quarterly, 21*(4), 360–407.

Stockton, F. R. (1882). The lady, or the tiger? *The Century, 25*(1), 83–86.

Successful Teachers. (2011, August 17). *Dancing definitions* [Video file]. Accessed at www .youtube.com/watch?v=Ul0wZ1ANWKw on May 10, 2016.

Sweeny, S. M., & Mason, P. A. (2011). *Research-based practices in vocabulary instruction: An analysis of what works in grades preK–12.* West Barnstable: Massachusetts Reading Association.

Tech in 2. (2014, November 12). *How to use Kahoot! in the classroom* [Video file]. Accessed at www.youtube.com/watch?v=BJ3Er1-tCMc on May 9, 2016.

Thurstone, L. L. (1946). Note on a reanalysis of Davis' reading tests. *Psychometrika, 11*(3), 185–188.

Tyson, K. A. (n.d.a). *Activities to use with the word wall or spelling words.* Accessed at www .learningunlimitedllc.com/wp-content/uploads/2012/10/Word-Wall-Word-Activities.doc on June 21, 2016.

Tyson, K. A. (n.d.b). *Top tips for word walls.* Accessed at www.learningunlimitedllc .com/wp-content/uploads/2012/12/Day-1-12-Days-12-Tools-Word-Walls-by-Dr.-Kimberly -Tyson-Learning-Unlimited.pdf on January 24, 2016.

Tyson, K. A. (2012a, December 13). *Alphaboxes graphic organizer {12 days: Tool 7}* [Blog post]. Accessed at www.learningunlimitedllc.com/2012/12/alphaboxes-graphic-organizer on January 1, 2016.

Tyson, K. A. (2012b, December 6). *Concept circles {12 days: Tool 2}* [Blog post]. Accessed at www.learningunlimitedllc.com/2012/12/concept-circles-vocabulary on December 12, 2015.

Tyson, K. A. (2012c, December 24). *Infographic: Anchored word learning strategy {12 days: Tool 11}* [Blog post]. Accessed at www.learningunlimitedllc.com/2012/12/infographic-anchored -word-learning-strategy on December 13, 2015.

Tyson, K. A. (2012d, December 17). *Pinterest cheat sheet {12 days: Tool 8}* [Blog post]. Accessed at www.learningunlimitedllc.com/2012/12/pinterest-cheat-sheet on June 21, 2016.

Tyson, K. A. (2012e, December 10). *Twitter cheat sheet {12 days: Tool 4}* [Blog post]. Accessed at www.learningunlimitedllc.com/2012/12/twitter-cheat-sheet-for-educators on June 21, 2016.

Tyson, K. A. (2013a, July 8). *5 easy steps to rockin' word walls* [Blog post]. Accessed at www .learningunlimitedllc.com/2013/07/5-steps-word-walls on December 26, 2015.

Tyson, K. A. (2013b, July 5). *5 simple steps for effective vocabulary instruction* [Blog post]. Accessed at www.learningunlimitedllc.com/2013/07/5-steps-vocabulary-instruction on January 23, 2016.

Tyson, K. A. (2013c, February 10). *21 digital tools to build vocabulary* [Blog post]. Accessed at www.learningunlimitedllc.com/2013/02/20-digital-tools-for-vocabulary on December 20, 2015.

Tyson, K. A. (2013d, December 18). *Cheat sheet: 101+ Twitter chat groups for educators {12 days of literacy}* [Blog post]. Accessed at www.learningunlimitedllc.com/2013/12/educator -twitter-chat-groups on May 10, 2016.

Tyson, K. A. (2013e, January 4). *A literacy-rich classroom supports the Common Core* [Blog post]. Accessed at www.learningunlimitedllc.com/2013/01/literacy-rich-environments-support -the-common-core-infographic on May 6, 2016.

Tyson, K. A. (2013f, May 26). *No tears for tiers: Common Core tiered vocabulary made simple* [Blog post]. Accessed at www.learningunlimitedllc.com/2013/05/tiered-vocabulary on January 23, 2016.

Tyson, K. A. (2013g, September 2). *Teacher toolkit: Tools and resources for educators.* Accessed at www.learningunlimitedllc.com/2013/09/teacher-toolkit-free-resources-for-educators on June 21, 2016.

Tyson, K. A., Cornwell, L., & Swetnam, R. (2009). *Zionsville School Corporation: The Literacy Lens comprehensive K–12 review—Final report.* Carmel, IN: Learning Unlimited.

Umphrey, J. (2008). Producing learning: A conversation with Robert Marzano. *Principal Leadership, 8*(5), 16–20.

Vacca, R. T., & Vacca, J. L. (1986). *Content area reading* (2nd ed.). Boston: Little, Brown.

Vagle, N. D. (2015). *Design in five: Essential phases to create engaging assessment practice.* Bloomington, IN: Solution Tree Press.

Wagner, R. K., Muse, A. E., & Tannenbaum, K. R. (Eds.). (2007). *Vocabulary acquisition: Implications for reading comprehension.* New York: Guilford Press.

Wilhelm, J. D. (2002). *Action strategies for deepening comprehension: Role plays, text-structure tableaux, talking statues, and other enactment techniques that engage students with text.* New York: Scholastic.

Wimmer, S. (2012). *The word collector* (J. Brokenbrow, Trans.). Madrid: Cuento de Luz.

Wolfersberger, M. E., Reutzel, D. R., Sudweeks, R., & Fawson, P. C. (2004). Developing and validating the classroom literacy environment profile (CLEP): A tool for examining the "print richness" of early childhood and elementary classrooms. *Journal of Literacy Research, 36*(2), 211–272.

Zwiers, J. (2014a). *Developing academic oral communication skills.* Accessed at www.jeffzwiers.org/oral-communication.html on January 23, 2016.

Zwiers, J. (2014b). *Opportunities to develop oral language.* Newark, DE: International Literacy Association.

Index

20 Literacy Strategies to Meet the Common Core
Elaine K. McEwan-Adkins and Allyson J. Burnett

With the advent of the Common Core State Standards, some secondary teachers are scrambling for what to do and how to do it. This book provides twenty research-based strategies designed to help students meet those standards and become expert readers.

BKF588

40 Reading Intervention Strategies for K–6 Students
Elaine K. McEwan-Adkins

This well-rounded collection of reading intervention strategies, teacher-friendly lesson plans, and adaptable miniroutines will support and inform your RTI efforts. Many of the strategies motivate all students as well as scaffold struggling readers. Increase effectiveness by using the interventions across grade-level teams or schoolwide.

BKF270

Using Technology to Enhance Reading
Edited by Timothy V. Rasinski, Kristine E. Pytash, and Richard E. Ferdig

Discover how technological resources can improve the effectiveness and breadth of reading instruction to build student knowledge. Read real-world accounts from literacy experts, and learn how their methods can be adapted for your classroom.

BKF608

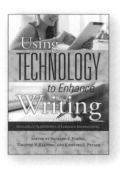

Using Technology to Enhance Writing
Edited by Richard E. Ferdig, Timothy V. Rasinski, and Kristine E. Pytash

Sharpen your students' communication skills while integrating digital tools into writing instruction. Loaded with techniques for planning and organizing writing, this handbook troubleshoots issues students face when writing in a printed versus digital context and teaches them how to read in multiple media.

BKF607

Solution Tree | Press
a division of
Solution Tree

Visit SolutionTree.com or call 800.733.6786 to order.

Wait! Your professional development journey doesn't have to end with the last pages of this book.

We realize improving student learning doesn't happen overnight. And your school or district shouldn't be left to puzzle out all the details of this process alone.

No matter where you are on the journey, we're committed to helping you get to the next stage.

Take advantage of everything from **custom workshops** to **keynote presentations** and **interactive web and video conferencing**. We can even help you develop an action plan tailored to fit your specific needs.

Let's get the conversation started.

Call 888.763.9045 today.

SolutionTree.com